YORKSHIRE'S
YAMMER

PETER WRIGHT

DALESMAN

Dalesman Publishing Company Ltd
Stable Courtyard, Broughton Hall,
Skipton, North Yorkshire BD23 3AE

First published 1994
Reprinted in this format 1997

© Dalesman Publishing Company Ltd

Cover illustration by Silvey Jex

A British Library Cataloguing in Publication record
is available for this book

ISBN 1 85568 077 7

Printed by Amadeus Press, Huddersfield

CONTENTS

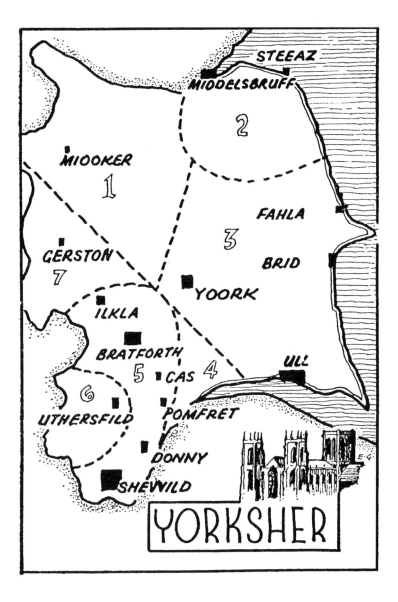

THE YORKSHIRE YAMMER

YOU CAN'T escape dialect. Most people think others talk it, not themselves, but it is everywhere. Even Standard English springs from a dialect (East Midlands) and, wherever two people try to speak the same language, dialects there must be. *Yammer* is from the Anglo-Saxon word *geomerian*, whose chief meaning has altered from "to mourn" into "make a constant loud noise" – and Tykes certainly make plenty of that.

Local dialect differs from slang in being serious and limited to a certain area. Thus, if you hear a person claim "E's off 'is nut/book/rocker", you sense that he is having a quiet laugh by slinging slang towards the poor victim, whereas if he says "E's off 'is 'eead" (or *yed* in some parts), it might be taken more seriously. This book therefore concentrates on Yorkshire's dialect, a miniature language with its own words, the antics of their semantics (word-meanings), pronunciation, grammar and so on – in other words on the delights of its dialect rather than the titillation and twang of slang.

Every Yorkshire locality has its own dialect, its cities using more of a mixture of the broad country dialects around them and Standard English. Nevertheless the main language border (see map) runs between areas 1-3 with their Northern dialects and areas 4-7 with their North Midland ones. Try explaining that to a Skiptonian or a *Barlicker*, but it's true! This is because in Anglo-Saxon times all England north of the Humber and Ribble spoke in a Northern dialect called Northumbrian, which survives in the North and East Ridings, whereas industrialisation has pushed up into the West Riding a North Midland form of speech, the type used for convenience in this book. The chief differences are:

	Northern		
Words like	*Area 1*	*Area 2*	*Area 3*
house	oos	oos	oos
spade	spyad	speead	speead
boots	beeats	beeats	beeats
speak	speeak	speeak	speeak
three	threr-ee	three	three
coal	cooal	cooal	cooal

North Midland

Words like	Area 4	Area 5	Area 6
house	ouse	ahs	ehs
spade	spehad	spehad	spade
boots	boots	booits	booits
speak	speeak	speyk	speyk
three	three	three	three
coal	cooal	coil	coil

Grammar also changes from place to place. Around Patrington they manage without *the,* saying not "into the cart" or even "into t'cart" but just "into cart". Here they are so independent that we may expect a nationalist movement in Holderness any day. Then instead of *she,* Huddersfield and Halifax traditionally say *oo* like southeast Lancashire; while Leeds, Bradford, Dewsbury and Keighley folk mix them and call her *shoo.*

Words change too. In different parts of Yorkshire cows are kep in a *coo-oos, cow-ouse, (cow) byre, shuppm, shippon, cow-shed, leeath* (lathe," i.e. barn plus cowhouse), *mistle and kah-oil.* Left-handed Yorkshiremen are rare; but plenty according to area are *keggy, kaggy, gallock-* or *doughy-anded, cuddy-fisted, kay-pawed* or *dolly-posh.* So, next time a motorist in front signals to turn left and veers right, you can rise to high local rhetoric with "Tha girt, gaumless, giggish, glaikit, gainless, gallock-anded gawk!"

Because the Vikings raided and settled in Yorkshire, we have many deeply-rooted Old Norse terms like *addle* "earn", *lake* "play", or "be off work", *ket* "rubbish", *baitin'* "snack" or *luggin' a poke* "pulling a sack", Dutch ones like *skipper* and *sketch,* French ones like *creeam* and *reeasty* "stubborn", one or two Latin ones like *auction* or *pob(bie)s* "child's soft food", those from other languages like *tay* and *whisky,* some from queer twists of pronunciation as with *eether* and *neether,* echoic words such as *jubber* "talk idiotically", and others of obscure origin like *dollop* "shapeless lump". Yet nine-tenths come from old native stock. "Yer gert cawf-eead!" or "Yon clatcan's waar not a clockin' 'en" ("that gossip's worse than a clocking hen") may sound odd but are all Anglo-Saxon words.

PLACE-NAMES AND PERSONAL NAMES

YORKSHIRE place-names can be pleasant-looking like Appletreewick, repulsive like Stanks, comical like Ugthorpe and Wetwang, apparently dangerous like Wressle and Skidby, carefree like Skipsea and Skipton, or short and odd like Heck, Hook, Jump, Shelf and Slack. Sometimes a smart residential district's name hides an embarrassing meaning, like Sheffield's Fulwood – "dirty wood", but seemingly distressing ones can be quite harmless, like Bugthorpe – "Buggi's village."

Most come from Anglo-Saxon, but as Yorkshire was part of the Danelaw there are many Scandinavian ones (e.g. those starting with the sound *sk-*). Celtic ones are few, but include the rivers Hodder, Calder, Esk and Wharfe. Horses appear in a few names, notably Horsforth (*'Ossfath* to a proper Tyke), Follifoot (from *foal*) and Rosedale (from Old Norse *hross* for a horse). The spelling often disguises the real name. The sign post may direct you to Skirlington, but you want one sounding like *skeleton*; it may say Great Ayton, whereas you seek *Yatton*.

A commercial traveller, lost near Helmsley, was told "Thoo's i' Airum" (rhyming with scarem). Excited by visions of ladics of the Middle East, he asked "How is it spelt?" "Thoo doesn't spell it" came the answer, "thoo ses it". Spelling Harome is evidently useless.

Here are other deceptive signs:

Apttrick – "Appletreewick"
Attic – "Atwick"
Borkby – "Birkby"
Bostwig – "Burstwick"
Brig(as) – "Brighouse"
Deeton – "Deighton"
Yelland – "Elland"
Gilswick – "Giggleswick"
Ezzle – "Hessle"
(Y)ebdin Brig or T'Brig – "Hebden Bridge"

Yakkam – "Acomb"
Bodsall – "Birdsall"
Bolland – "Bowland"
Bohmer – "Bulmer"
Shivvan – "Chevin"
Eeasynud – "Easingwold"
Flehmbrer – Flamborough"
Go-car – "Golcar"
Ipram – "Hipperholme"

Utton Panel – "Hooton Pagnell"	*Umpton* – "Holmpton"
Awzam – "Halsham"	*Oscar* – "Hawsker"
Keethla/Keythla – "Keighley"	*Kennigam* – "Keyingham"
Killick Peearcy – "Kilnwick Percy"	*Linfit* – "Linthwaite"
Laatle Weeton – "Little Weighton"	*Mawm* – "Malham"
Mawtby – "Maltby"	*Mask* – "Marske"
Awd Mawton - "Old Malton"	*Pehatla Brig* – "Pateley Bridge"
Rushworth – "Rishworth"	*Rivvis or Rivers* – "Rievaulx"
Slawit or Slow-wit – "Slaithwaite"	*Sawby Brig* – "Sowerby Bridge"
Tordmin – "Todmorden"	*Wummersla* – "Womersley"
Rawby – "Wragby"	*Yeeadon* – "Yeadon"

Mind you, some Yorkshiremen have a bizarre view of dwelling-places. Visitors seeking an elderly native were told by the first man they asked, "Nay, Ah's an off-cummed-'un." "From where?" they insisted. "From away," he logically replied. They stopped another. "Have you lived here all your life, my man?" "Not yit." Anxiously they tried a third. "Nay," he answered, "Ah were born i' Masham" (two miles away but in another Riding), adding, "Ah wish Ah noo wheer Ah was to dee, an' then Ah'd keep well cleear o' that spot."

Place-name sayings are not always to the county's good. To "come Yorkshire" over anyone is to cheat him; to "give Scarborough warning" is to give none at all; and "to do a Shevild" is to run away. Most places mentioned come out badly in the rhyme; "Bradford for cash, Halifax for dash, Wakefield for pride and poverty; 'Uthersfild for show, Sheffield what's low, Leeds for dirt and vulgarity." Another one is "Huddersfield for worth, Leeds costs the earth."

Here are some more:
Great Ayton: Yattoners wade over t'beck to save t'brig.
Hackness: "All of a sahd, like Ackniss Fair" (which was held on a hillside).
Halifax, etc: "From Hell, Hull and Halifax, good Lord deliver us."
"Halifax is build of wax, Heptonstall of stooan;
I'Halifax there's bonny lasses, i'Heptonstall there's nooan."
Hallamshire: "When all the world shall be aloft,
Then Hallamshire shall be God's croft."

Harrogate: "Said t'Devil when flyin' ower Harrogate wells,
"I think I'm getting home by the smells."
Hull, etc: "As strong as Hull."
Oxford for leaning, London for wit,
Hull for women, and York for a tit (horse).
Ingleborough, etc: "Ingleborough, Pendle and Pen-y-ghent
Are the highest hills between Scotland and Trent."
Kippax: "Wheer they put a wire fence rahnd it to keep t'fog aht."
Leeds, etc: "To go rahnd bi Leeds an' Otla."
i.e. to make a long-winded statement.
Marsden: "Wheer they put t'pigs on t'wall to listen to t'band.
Ossett: "Wheer they black-leaded t'tram-lines."
Pontefract: "As sure as a louse in Pomfret."
Pudsey: "Wheer all good cricketers come from."
"Wheer t'ducks fly back'ards."
Roseberry: "When Roseberry Topping wears a cap,
Let Cleveland then beware a clap" (downpour).
Sheffield: "When Sheffield Park is ploughed and sown,
Then little England hold thine own."
Slaithwaite: "Slow-wit, wheer they raked t'mooin aht o'tcut"
(or rather, tried to rake its reflection out of the canal).
Wharfedale and Airedale: Wharfe is clear and Aire is lithe,
Where the Aire drowns one, Wharfe drowns five."
York: "Lincoln was, London is, but York shall be
The greatest city of the three."

Street names are also fascinating. The *gate of Briggate, Fargate,* etc., is from an Old Norse word for way. York's *Shambles* is from open-air stalls from which meat was sold, and its *Whip-ma-Whop-ma-Gate* doubtless alludes to the whipping post and pillory that were at the end of the street, while Halifax's *Gibbet Street* is from the gibbet or guillotine it led to. Any Yorkshire locality provides an interesting crop of names. For instance, Leeds includes the districts *Chapiltahn* "Chapeltown", *Kirstall* "Kirkstall", *Meeanwood, Rahndeh* and *'Unslit,* the thoroughfares *Briggit* and *Kirgit* – "Kirkgate"; and *Aaron's Lane* – "Harehills Lane," but *Booar Loin* and *Woodus Loin* – "Woodhouse Lane."

Of course, not everyone is happy with his address: Thus,

for example, Baildon's exquisite name *Mudd Lane* graces envelopes no more.

Yorkshire birthplaces give remarkable nicknames. Besides the general term *Tyke*, there are more precisely *Leeds Loiners*, *Go-car* ("Golcar") *Lilies, Barlickers,* etc.; but *Morley Gawbies* have disowned their name and have foisted it onto other Morleys outside Yorkshire. Then soccer fans will recognise the *Owls* and *Blades*; rugby league followers the *Fartowners* and *Robins*; speedway enthusiasts the *Tigers*; and so on.

From Yorkshire places arise many surnames, such as Ashcroft, Batley, Bentley, Braithwaite, Bramley, Cawthorne, Crosland, Dent, Garforth, Haworth, Helmsley, Holdsworth, Leeming, Liversage, Lockwood, Malton, Midgley, Pickering, Rippon, Roscoe, Scholes, Staniland, Tatham. If your name is there, take pride in being an absolute Yorkshireman; even if it isn't, don't worry – the full list is longer.

Then there are individual nicknames. A large village near Leeds boasted, among others, a *Red'Un, Pullet, Jumbo, Peepy Duck, Pot Egg, Tripe Eead and Cauf Tommy* – jovial coinages. *Ahr* is a distinguishing feature – *ahr Tom, ahr Alice,* and so on. It is useful in large families where you have to distinguish yours from others' Toms, Alices. It has nicer ramifications, as when you refer, *snotty-nooased-like*, to *their* Alice.

NANCY
METCALFE

"Ah've telled thee abaht standin' an' yammerin' i' this sooart o' weather."

YORKSHIRE CHARACTERISTICS

THE WORDS they use suggest that Yorkshire folk are a very pugnacious breed. If angered, they are likely to *belt, bensill, bray, lace, leather, pawse* ("kick") or *skelp* you, or for variety will "gie tha thi bats," "gie tha a claht over t'eead," "fetch tha a kelt over t'shoothers," or "mek thi brains rattle."

Again, their language suggests that their ranks contain an unfortunate array of idiots. Some are apparently "as daft as muck" or "as daft as a scuttle," "as fond as a turnip," "as gawmless as a suckin' duck" or "three sheets to t'wind"; whilst the slightly less foolish are just *silly gobbins*. Naturally, not all Yorkshire natives are brain-boxes. One *missus* came home with wood for a new clothes prop and asked *t'mester* to cut the cleft for her. "Aye," he said, "wheer's t'prop?" "Leeanin' up agen t'ahs wall." "Then Ah'll borrer a stee" ("ladder"), he said. "Tha cracked fooil!" she retorted, "what's wrang wi' sawin' it fra' t'bedroom winder?" There was, too, the *lurry drahver* observed frantically trying to claw down the stonework of an arch which his vehicle could not quite pass underneath. "Why don't you let your tyres down a bit?" asked a helpful passer-by. "Nay," answered the stupid driver, "it's t'lurry roof 'at wain't go under, not t'wheels."

Drunkeness also causes many assessments like "as drunk as fuzzocks," "as drunk as a newt" or "as drunk as a sweep." Some Tykes are apparently so mean that they will *tek t'theeat aht o' thi mustard*, and, as is well-known, the Great Hortoners will *nip a corran* ("current") i' two. Untidy women abound, judging by all the *slatterns, trollops, slovens,* and *tosspots* whose houses are a proper *snipperty*; and an incredible number of gossips, busybodies, *clat-cans* and *toots* with all their *callin', campin'* (without tents) and *tootin'* ("She were rahnd 'ere again tootin' this mornin'") But don't be alarmed; all these descriptions arise because such people excite pointed comment in all cultures.

The typical Tyke can be very defensive in shifting the blame. A Wolds farmer riding his *'oss* with his wife walking wearily behind was asked, "Why ain't thi missus ridin'?", to be answered, "Shoo esn't nooa 'oss." Another native, reminded by a Cleveland magistrate, "You were brought in by two police drunk, I suppose", agreed "Aye, yer reverence, they was." Above all, the Tyke is very sensitive about his speech. One reproved a Cockney, "Any road" (anyway), "we say things proper, a *cup o' tay* or by its letters a *cup o' teea*, not a *cap o' tie* like you lot."

The Yorkshireman and his dealect are supposedly blunt. Even his so-called abstract nouns are anything but abstract in meaning; e.g. *gumption* or the Greek word *nous* for sense ("e's got nooa nous"); or *guts* and *spunk* for bravery or determination. Yorkshire people are realistic. "What an adorable view!" exclaimed a visitor. "Aye," grunted the dales farmer, "but it weeant pay t'rent." His neighbour added, "We've nowt but scenery an' thoo caan't see that for t'ills." Arthur Jarratt relates the tale that a farm labourer, hearing frantic cries from a man up to his neck in a deep pond, asked, "What's thi name?" "John Robinson from Bielby's Farm," said the man, "an Ah can't hodd aht mich longer." Ignoring him, the labourer rushed to the farm and asked the foreman, "Dusta know John Robinson's drahndin'?" "What abaht it?" said the foreman "Ah've come for his job." "Tha's ower late. We've gin it to t'chap 'at chucked 'im in."

Often, though, bluntness is partly a defence. Under the rough manners and speech lies kindliness, but you must not show it for fear of looking "soft." And far better to qualify a success, so that folk will stay sympathetic towards you. The technique is easy. If they ask about your recovery from illness, you reply, "Ah might just mucky another cleean shirt".

Certain Yorkshire words act as maids-of-all-work. *Fettle* is one of these. You can, for instance, fettle ("mend") a fire, be *i'fahn fettle* ("condition"), or retort, "If tha ses that again, Ah'll sooin fettle thi." Another is *maul*. It can mean to meet a difficulty (Harassed mothers are *mauled abaht wi' t'kids*), to frequent ("Tha'll awlus fahnd 'im maulin abaht t'Bulls Yed"), or to associate with ("E's maulin abaht wi' that big lass aht 'a Canal Street"). An intricate task is *maulin'* and so is a very heavy one.

Nowt is another popular word, e.g. "It's just summat an' nowt," "E talks an ses nowt," "nowt said needs no mendin'," and the famous West Riding commandment, "See all, hear all, say nowt; eyt all, sup all, pay nowt; and if ivver that does owt for nowt, then do it for thisen."

One reason for the language mixture is that Yorkshire words can change at different rates. Thus in Castleford schoolchildren's speech in the last generation *thee* and *thou* have been rapidly disappearing but *us* as in "We'll ger us (our) books" is far more resilient.

Another snag is that every Yorkshire person has several layers of speech. He won't talk quite the same to the vicar, to a baby, and to a workmate who drops a paving slab on his toe. Politeness can turn a good Anglo-Saxon technical term like the *arse-end* into the *bottom* of a net; the normal *Eh?* into *What?* or *Pardon?*; an orthodox *belly* or *bally* into *stummick* or even *tummy*. What a pity that folk should try to talk *peys* ("peas") above sticks when Yorkshire speech has such potential! For instance, take (if you must) the terminology of the Queensbury beer barrel, which is made by a *tubber* or *tub-thumper*, and has a *shive* ("bung") into which you put the *spile-peg, garths* ("hoops"), *pitch* ("widest diameter"), etc. There really is no end to it – expressive Yorkshire vocabulary, not the barrel.

"No gaffer, I niver gits tired, cos I hev a rest when I feel it comin' on!"

HOW FAST DO YOU TALK?

INVESTIGATIONS INTO how many revs per minute the Tyke gives his *tung* have been driving devoted researchers up the wall. There are questions like whether women talk more than men and whether all the *yer knaws*, *yer sees* and *sithas* count as meaningful conversation or as forced muscle spasms. Such space-fillers can be useful in – er – giving you a second to think, but, *yer knaw-like*, don't overdo them. But the basic problem is that the Yorkshireman has three ways of communicating. He can, it seems, sleep most of the time with his eyes open but when needed make suitable signs and gestures, e.g. if he spots *townies* trampling through his cornfield. This works, as does dropping into conversations short comments like *Aye, Nay, Oh! Um!* or *Happen* ("perhaps"). A thoughtful exchange of views would be, e.g. "Did tha?" "Aye." "Yer nivver!" "Yigh ("Yes"), Ah did." "By!" The third way is to mash your words together and squelch the lot out at your listeners. Translate these, first covering the right-hand column so that you don't cheat. Please forgive us if the bunches of Yorkshire spelling look silly, but that is roughly how they would be heard by a tape recorder. The maximum score per line depends on its number of local words. One mark for each of them correctly understood:

Score	Standard Yorksher	Standard English
4	SHINTIN	The lady is not at home.
4	OOTELLDITIM?	Who told him?
4	WAREE WEISSEN?	Was he by himself?
5	ABURRISBAHT	Oh, but his mental capacities are in question.
4	AHSTHIMUM?	How is your mother?
4	WORARTYEVIN?	Would you care for a drink?
5	THAMUNGERRITETTN	You must eat it.
6	YALATTAGERROFF	You will have to dismount.
7	GERRIMTERGITHIAPOW	Get him to give you a haircut.
8	GIZZITNGERRAHTNIT	Give it me and go.

PITFALLS

HERE ARE some of the worst traps a non-settler meets:

1. Some natives always greet you with *Nah then!* as if you have been guilty of something. Take no notice, apart from replying with an encouraging mutter.

2. Many ordinary-looking Yorkshire words are tricky. A *dead good 'un* can be very much alive. Ossett and *ossin'* have *nowt* to do with horses, and Adel does not refer to eggs. If *pined*, you are not lamenting but feeling hungry; if *gegged* or *clammed,* your mouth is not shut but wide open because you are so thirsty; if *off yer meyt*, you want no food at all, not just meat; if *perished*, you are still alive though very cold; and, if a lass is *starved*, she is not ravenous – *utch up* to her, it's warmth she needs.

3. Rushing words or trying to cope with awkward learned words causes mistakes obvious to all but the speaker, like *obstrokolus* for the very hard to deal with and *parlatic* for too drunk to stand up. Others are *caterpillar* ("capilliary") *action*, *Ah've a Barnsla accident* ("accent"), *Yon's t'ospital insultant*, *At t'Ysterical Society*. Also, e.g. "we're workin' in collision," "women are gettin' too emaciated," "ahr Bill's marryin' a typewriter," "Sally's quite uninhabited," "tha can't do that theer, tha'll be ostrichised," "Ah were left-handed, but now Ah'm ambiguous." Don't laugh, for something similar will no doubt happen to you.

4. Don't put on a *Setdy neet voice*. We need no aitches. Flustered speakers who spurt them out at random, like "Boys hand girls, Hi ham 'appy to hopen this 'ere hanniversary," are too generous. And don't indulge in absurdities like *clahss* and *lahsst*, so beloved by *t'telly-lads*. Yorkshire talk loses its vigour when it becomes *quate refayned*.

5. Don't think that all those who *thou* and *thee* you are highly religious.

6. Watch *yersens* with *-sell* and *-sen*. North of *Gerston* ("Grassington") use *-sell,* south of it prefer *-sen*, around the border mix 'em.

WIMMIN

YORKSHIRE *wimmin* are reputed to cook substantial meals; to be interminably *fettlin'* their houses; speaking their minds sharp and hot; looking suspicious but treating friends very generously; not reckoning *over mich* for all that *muck* that cosmetically-inclined ladies feel bound to use; and wearing *kegs* in their hair all day long. Many were brought up in tougher times. The *slapstooan*, that shallow brown earthenware sink, used to have to be so zealously cleaned with abrasives that it became a very efficient collector of soapy and fatty scum, whose removal demanded more abrasives – and so on. But each is a person in her own right, and so many are *bonny, nahs-lookin', smart, flash,* or *fair stunners* that Yorkshire's beauty is well proved.

It has been claimed that no courting takes place in Yorkshire, and that there are only two processes, *tekkin' 'er aht* and *gooin' steady*. Certainly courting was taboo on Friday, because then there was so much inside housework such as *black-leeadin'* to be done. *Cooartin'* seems to be a general polite word for a situation involving several stages like *ossin' baht do* – "trying unsuccessfully," *chattin' 'er up, datin' 'er, bein' on t'arm* or *walkin' 'er aht,* and being *on a promise* – "engaged," which leads to *gerrin' wed* or *gerrin' spliced.*

The very common *woman* still seems widely acceptable, e.g. "E's gor a woman over i' Barnsla." Though it makes a stranger want to edge out of the room, like *botherin' wi'* it is just another substitute for courting. For "living in sin," besides *livin' over t'latch* there is the strangely righteous term *livin' Hallelujah.*

It is the Yorkshireman's common belief that, though his *missus* is expert at cooking and bringing up *t'bairns,* mechanically she cannot cope. As proof, cases are cited like that of the unlucky woman stuck in the rush hour at the Headrow traffic lights, and frantically trying to engage gear – any gear. A *bobby* rapped on her mini-car roof to enquire, "Nah, madam, ev wi no colour you do like?" And in Bradford they had a driver so *gaumless* that, when told her engine was missing, she started to look for it. For safety, we'd better leave the battle of the sexes.

T'BAIRNS

EXPERTS SAY that the best test of a dialect's resilience is how far children go on using it. If so, Yorkshire's dialect has a long future. Just listen to the speech in any playground when *skooil loises*. Some of the bright ones are bi-lingual and make able translators between their parents and visitors from remote places, but most are happier yapping in the Yorkshire yammer. It is heartening to report that the local speech is making new converts. A Bradford teacher of an immigrant class went to considerable trouble to learn a little Urdu, but when trying it out on the class was met by *Yer-what?*

The Yorkshire *bairn* has a hard time at *skooil*, where they try to *larn* him to spell *tayters* with a p, to start *lectrik* with an e, etc. Infant *reeadin'* books have been made unnecessarily puzzling through refusing to employ the Initial Yorkshire Alphabet, which is:

A for *osses*, B for lamb, C for thissen, D for and deeper, E for Adam, F for ready, G for police, H for starting work, I for a *fahn lass*, J for oranges, K for mines, L for leather, M for sis, No for eggs, O for Yorkshire pud, P for Pudsey, Q for *nowt* R for second, S for *esta?*, T for *warchin'*, U for *getten*, V for victory, W for a *pahnd*, X for sale, Y for kids, Z for *t'doctor*.

Non-Tykes may require a translation. A: Hay for horses. B: Beef or lamb. C: See for yourself. D: Deeper and deeper. E: Eve or Adam. F: Ever-ready. G: Chief of Police. H: Age for starting work. I: Eye for a fine girl. J: Jaffa oranges. K: Kaffir mines. L: Hell for leather. M: Emphasis. N: Hen for eggs. O: Oh for Yorkshire pudding. P: –. Q: Queue for nothing. R: Half a second. S: have you? T: Teeth are aching. U: You've forgotten. V: –. W: Double you for a pound. X: Eggs for sale. Y: Wife or kids. Z: Send for the Doctor.

Great hopes, however, are pinned on the staff at County *Eddication Office*, who are reportedly considering the introduction Mr. F.A. Carter's West Riding Alphabet, which starts:

"A is for apple 'at Eve yarked off t'Tree," and continues:
"K is for kids wi' sich owd buck an' cheek,
You feel yo' could poise 'em reight into next week.
L is for livin' at 's nooan allis fun,

But it's better nor deein' when all's said an' done.
M is for muck; yo' can turn up yer nooase,
But it meks yer peys grow, an' puts beauty i't'rooase ...,

Yorkshire bairns enjoy sucking *claggy goodies, bullets* or *spahs*, but hate *weshin' theirsens*, being ready to leave a *mucky tahd-mark* round their necks. They are reluctant to comb their hair, so that it gets *cottery, matted, tousled, rough towy* or *luggy*. They chant, "Ooh he is a sooly kid, dirty as a dustbin lid," noticing their friend's grime but not their own.

With modern medicine they suffer less from illnesses like *t'mazzles*, but still need plenty of watching. The best way is to *keep 'em i'toit* ("busy"). If they are *marlockin'* ("getting up to mischief"), the traditional swift punishment of *jartin* their *backsides* or giving them a *claht on t'lug-oil* is better than just scolding or *snahpin'* at them. Otherwise they will get up to further pranks, like tying together door knobs of adjacent houses or playing *divvil up a spaht*, where paper is stuffed up a rainwater down-spout and lit to make a weird noise; and they will turn cheeky, *lapin'* or *slakin' their tung* out at you.

Their games are changing rapidly as the Yorkshire street scene changes owing to traffic and shifting families. Popular games used to include *'op-flag* – "hop-scotch," *duckstooan, knurr an'spell, tip-cat* (where a tin on a string was whirled round), *bell horses* for the girls, whip-and-top, cigarette card games like *babby* or *chap*, or *skim on*, and the team jumping game called *truss-weight* or *ah monny fingers up?*

Marbles or *merpies* was played in four ways. These were the ring game; the hole game, called *bungums, bunhole* or *knuck(le)*; the line game; and the game of *hundreds*. Marbles were named from the material (e.g. *clayey, chalky*), appearance (*ginger, blood alley*), worth (*twentier*), or function (*shooter, chuck, knuck*). The games had a whole vocabulary of their own, like *drakes, dregs* or *bize* for the base line; *Bally me this!* for claiming a marble; and *shank* for losing them all. The worst crimes were to steal marbles or *scrab*, and to cheat by moving your hand forward when shooting, called *skinchin'* or *fudge-juckin'*. Considering such lively games and minor offences against modern canned entertainment and vandalism, it looks as if we have lost "the good old days."

FOOD AND DRINK

GRUB IS relished in the White Rose county and it is customary and polite to show it. You must *gollop* it, and *guzzle, gaunch, slubber, slowp, slotch, slop* or *sozzle* your drink, even though this makes you a *sluther-guts*.

The Tyke scoffs at dieting and is contemptuous of *rabbit food* ("salad"), *milestooan puddin'* with a mile between each currant, and flat-rib, a type of cheap mild beer. He hates *Resurrection Day,* when Sunday leftovers are recooked; and continually craves *summat t'eyt*, not because it is delicately arranged or politely served, *but to do me good*. This is how you make his most illustrious dish:

Recipe for Yorkshire Pud

"Tha wants a quarter pahnd o' flahr, a big Yorkshire oyster ("egg"), 'awf a tablespoon o' drippin, 'awf a pahnt o' milk an' a bit o'sawt ("salt"). Mix t'flahr an' sawt in a basin, mek a oller i't'middle an' breyk yer oyster i' that. Add two tablespoons o' milk, an' stir in some o'tflahr wi' a thible ("wooden spoon"). Keep on till tha's used awf t'milk. Beeat it 5 minits an' let it stand for 20, then eeat t'drippin' in a bakin' tin. Put t'rest o't'milk into t'batter an' teem it into a 'ot dish. Bake it 30 minits, cur it into two-inch squers, an' start gobblin".

"Impooartant: Eyt it afoor t'main cooarse. When tha sarves it, say, "Them at eyts mooast puddin' 'll get mooast meyt," so as, when they're stawed up ("full") wi t'pud, they'll not want mich else."

When food was scarce, a number of put-offs were used when children asked what there was to eat, such as "tunes and buttered haycocks," "few broth," "nowt warmed up." But when *brass* was more plentiful, great and glorious dishes arrived – simnel cake for Mothering Sunday, Spotted Dick, broth and dumplings, *urrins* (once ten a penny) fried in oatmeal, home-made sly cake, pig's cheek, crab salad ... What we have lost in the modern rush of life!

SPOOART

THE TYKE has an almost pathological interest in football. There is a Northern saying, "Shaht down t'pit, an' up'll come a footballer." So watch yersens *on t'causa* ("pavement") and board up your shops if he's late for Elland Road or Odsal, or if his team *loises*. It makes him mad to hear how much publicity goes to other teams when all the good ones are clustered east of the Pennines. Yet he keeps getting embroiled in senseless civil wars.When *t'Owls* play *t'Blades*, the Army is put on stand-by; and all police leave is cancelled when Featherstone *punc* and *bensill* Cas. in the filthy mud.

Round these trial meeting places fly interesting comparisons.Of rugby league three-quarters too often tackled from behind, it will be said, "Ah thowt yon mon were fast. He's fast to t'floor!" Some have extended beyond sport. "Ah feel a bit offsahd today" must have come from football, though it only means you aren't well.

The Tyke has, of course, many other vital sporting interests, like fishing, ten-pin bowling, and a certain summer game well-known to Freddie Trueman, Boycott & Co., but for a change let us consider pigeon-fancying, where also it is the technique that matters. For best results you put one of your best *homers* out as a *strag* – "stray pigeon" into someone else's *stragoil* ("loft"), where it gets friendly with the residents, inevitable among these amiable but gullible birds. Then you *clap yer pigeon 'ooam again* and some of its new friends will follow it, whereupon you calmly lock them up in your own *strag-oil*. From this comes another term which has extended beyond the normal bounds of sport, for *straggin'* now stands also for the process of picking up a girl.

If sporting skill will not itself win for you, there are fortunately other ways. One is to accuse opponents of cheating. For instance, if a man plays a wrong domino, you interrupt, "Eigh, own abaht, owt abaht! (roughly, "What's the matter?) Tha knocked on nines last time!" If defeat cannot be hidden there is the common excuse, especially in billiards, snooker and darts, "Ah'd not getting' mi een ("eyes") in."

YORKSHIRE SPEYKS
(PROVERBS AND COMPARISONS)

THE YORKSHIREMAN is quick to spot a likeness, which is why he is so fond of proverbs and special sayings. He is rarely *gobsmacked* – "dumb-founded" – though he won't waste breath repeating good sense to a stupid listener. Many of these proverbial sayings concern animals. Thus: "E's browt 'is pigs to a fine market," said of a man who has caused his downfall by drink, gambling, crime or too much womanising, "as wick ("quick") as an eel"; "mutton dressed up as lamb," e.g. of a 60-year-old in a mini-skirt; "dressed up lahk a dog's dinner" or "tha's wuss nor a dog i' an entry" ("alleyway"), a comment on a persistent arguer or a nagging wife; "e's tight' ("mean"), it's lahk gerrin' muck from a wooden 'oss."

Some, like the last, are a wee bit exaggerated. Similarly: "as faws ("false") as a cartload o' monkeys'; "as sick as a parrot"; "E's double-fisted but threpple-throited," of someone skilled with his hands but too fond of drink.

Some local *speyks* have to be modified. Thus "Look afoor yer lowp ("before you leap") an' dooan't awlus lowp"; "wheer there's muck there's brass ("money") but mooast on it ("most of it") gooas on fettlin" (maintenance).

Here are some more comparisons to increase your repertoire: "as straight as a loith (spindle)"; as daft as a dish-claht"; "as deead as a coffin-nail"; "as foul as a ripped clog"; "as black as t'fire-back"; "E's weel hefted wi' brass", i. e. has plenty of money; "awlus i't field when 'e should be i't'loin", of someone never ready when opportunity knocks; "nawther reyt poised (kicked) nor unpoised", of anyone always dissatisfied; "prick one an' they all bleed", of tightly-knit Yorkshire communities.

You may need the support of a few extra proverbs: "awlus be i't'foor-end of a feeast and t'latter end of a fray"; "etten jock's sooin forgettin", of ungrateful people; "brass tekken aht o' thi pocket is moor nor 'awf (more than half) spent", "if a man thinks e's weel off, e's weel off"; "mak t'best o'things-even t'mester (your husband)".

BELIEFS AND CUSTOMS

Birth, etc: If a mother rocks an empty cradle, or if you sell your pram, another *babby* will come; stepping over a crawling *babby* will stop it getting on in life; cutting its fingernails will make it a thief.

Weddings: With a piece of wedding cake under her pillow, a lady will dream of her future husband; "Change the name and not the letter, you wed for wuss an' not for better."

Bad Luck: From *booits* on the table or an *oppen umbrella* in the house.

Death: People die (from natural causes) always on the ebb tide. Death portents are a clock stopping for no reason, a robin tapping at a window, or fruit and flowers appearing together on a tree.

"Ollerdies": Before going away, put 50 pence under the clock to make sure there will be enough *brass* left for when you come back.

"Fooitins": A party or trip where all help to *fooit* the bill. But folk who 20 years ago had *fooitins* now go to classy restaurants. This change in life styles is the real danger to many words, not the B.B.C. or Standard English. It is only when you do different things that the old words and meanings go.

Directions: The Tyke's customary ways of directing strangers shoulds be treated cautiously. He may say, "See yon church past t'crossroads? Well, it's not that rooad ... " He may refer to demolished landmarks like Turner's Garage because he still seems to see them and can't believe they have gone. His distances may be awry, either through calculating in the *Yorkshire mile* or through politics – e.g. he may find it hard to direct you from Bentham to Hawes in another Riding, and almost impossible to guide you to *Lankyster*, which is foreign soil.

YORKSHIRE CURES

Note.- Several of these have been proved very effective, but not all are guaranteed and a few leave rather a niff.

Ailment	Cure
sooir throit	Blow sulphur down it from a paper funnel, or rub it with *gooisgreease,* or wrap *yer left-'and stockin'* round it.
warts	Sell them to someone else, tie them with horsehair, or bury in the ground a piece of steak. As it decomposes, the warts fade.
arthuritis	Bathe with boiled sea-water and bandage with seaweed.
bad back	Wear a red flannel belt.
poor eyesight	Pierce *yer lugs*
lugwarch	Fasten half a roasted onion next to *t'lug* with a *muffler*.
ordinary cough	Tie round *t'throit* in a muslin bag a live hairy caterpillar.
chink-cough	*Rooast otchin* ("hedgehog"), *frahd mahs* or a live *tooad* held close to *t'gob* to suck the cough out; or put your *eyd* over a hot tar-barrel.
sprained wrist	Wrap it with eelskins.
bally-warch	Drink *cider-tay.*
screwmatics	Wear a brass ring, or put a nutmeg or *tayter* in your left *wesket* pocket, or try *knit-booan*.
cramp *at neet*	Take a *tayter* to bed with you.
a boil	Press over it a heated narrow-nicked bottle. In theory, the pressure of the cooling bottle drawn out the *matter*. Agonising in practice.
englarged breast	Apply *a cow-pack*.

For owt, a remedy claimed is alcohol. From peasants to kings the faith in it persists. People with slipped discs and others with raging hangovers have drunk brandy and port. The only sensible attitude is that of the near-alcoholic who refused whisky for a heavy cold, saying "Not ruddy lahkly. Booze is mi pleasure."

TRANSLATIONS

TRUE YORKSHER has been used, believe it or not, for conversion direct into the universal language. Esperanto without belittling itself by going through Standard English, to translate parts of the Bible and for short graces. One grace sometimes used at school meals runs, "For every cup and plateful, Lord make us truly grateful." Parallel and without disrespect is the older Yorkshire version, "Fatther, fill mi mahth wi' worthwhile stuff, An' nudge me when Ah've etten enough."

OTHER LANGUAGE ODDITIES

VERY ODD are the paradoxes, where the earnest Tyke seems to contradict himself. Examples: "E talks an' ses nowt", i.e. is not worth hearing; "thoo's mended it wahr" ("worse"), e.g. of darning a sock too roughly; "it's summat an' nowt" ("unimportant"); "Ah caan't see for lookin'", "next time Ah bring yo two to t'shops, Ah'll leeave yer at whom" ("home").

Very similar are those where a *mum* asks of her child the impossible. E.g. "Tha's reet mucky ("quite dirty"). Just look i'thi lug ("ear")!" – hard without a mirror; "dusta want a smack?" – no child says "Yes"; "if tha doesn't come in, that wain't gooa aht again"; "shut thi gob ("mouth") an' eyt thi dinner up."

Spoonerisms, where parts of words interchange, occasionally appear and are caused by talking too fast and thinking of the words ahead. E.g. flutterbyes "butterflies"; "Tek thi cat flap ("flat cap")"; "spy an' puds ("pie and spuds")"; "pledge an' wires ("wedge and pliers")"; "bend yon mike ("mend that bike"); "dust in ivvery crook an' nanny ("nook and cranny")." So unusual do they sound that the poor Tyke's speech accident brings his listeners up with a jerk.

'MATHERMATICKS'

THE *Guinness Book of Records* states that there is a tribe which meets any attempt to convey the idea of more than three with total stupefaction. Despite contrary arguments, it is not in Yorkshire. Many an old Dales farmer, whom outsiders believe can hardly count, has his own system far more reliable than any computer. As, however, alternative examination syllabuses are now in force, our approach covers both old methods and new.

Owd Maths: This survives chiefly in memories of old Celtic sheep-scoring numerals, of which there were several systems:

	1	2	3	4	5
Airedale	era	tera	tethera	fethera	pimps
Swaledale	yan	tean	tethera	methera	mick
Nidderdale	yehn	tehn	edura	pedura	pips
Ribblehead	yah	twa	thethera	methera	pimp

Compare Keswick – yan, twan, tether, mether, pimp; and Welsh – un, dau, tri, pedwar, pump. The Ribblehead count went up to 49, which was *cracker buck;* the others stopped at 20.

Yet in 1950 in Muker, late one evening when Professor Harold Orton and I were watching shepherds playing dominoes in the small tap-room of the inn we had made our dialect base, he pointed out that they were using sheep-scoring language. How sad that, comparatively inexperienced as I then was, I made no notes of it, for Muker could have embraced its last genuine survival in England!

Modern Maths: To multiply 6 pigs by 8 – ger a booar.

If it wern't fer summat, there'd be nowt. Umpteen is a gert lot.

If yer buys a score o' tayters fer a pahnd an' sells 'em fer two, that's nobbut wun per cent profit.

Two minuses meks a plus, three on 'em meks a bigger plus – there's nivver nowt nooa surer.

To fahnd rooits, dig up a tree.

Twelve inch meks wun fooit, three fooit meks wun yard, three thousand yard meks a Yorkshire mahl.

Sometimes, admittedly, arithmetical mistakes occur. A Hull

builder submitted an estimate of £222,222.22 for his three sons and himself to dig a tunnel under the Humber with pick and shovel, two working from each side. When asked what would happen if the two sections failed to meet, he replied, "Then tha'll get two for t'prahs o'wun." At other times, however, Yorkshire reckoning is most exact. One customer, after vainly trying to describe the ice-cream he wanted, was curtly told, "You mean a 99, mate." Next week he asked for a "495." "Whatever's that?" asked the baffled salesman. Quick came the answer, "Five 99s."

Definitions: Simple interest – what any fooil can add up; integration – what tha'es i'Bratforth; similar figures – them wi' t'same curves; squers – owd fashioned fooak; prism – Armley Gaol; factor – 'im 'at works in a factory; logs – what yer chop; circle – straight lahn bent rahnd to meet itsen wi' a oil i't'middle; sine – what yer mek wi' yer 'ands; cosine – oppnin' call ont' wireless; tangent – what some fooak go off at.

"Tell me, is that bull safe?"
"Ee's a lot safer ner three, mate."

26

ANIMALS

WEIRDLY-NAMED animals are common in Yorkshire. Insects include the arran that spins an *arran-web,* the *clock* for any kind of beetle, *twitch-bell* for earwig, and for a centipede the unmathematical *forty-leg.* Wherever flies are *fleas,* fleas understandably are something else, usually *lops.* Birds include *pyenot* – "magpie"; *spuggy, spadger* or *Dicky dunnock* – "sparrow"; *peewit* or *tewit* – "lapwing"; and *shepsters* or *sheppies* – "starlings." Likewise the names of bigger animals may surprise city dwellers. A sheep may be, according to age and sex, a *tup, teeap* or *tewp, yowe, hog, hoggit* or *gimmer*; and it is alleged that, when a Dalesman becomes a proud father, the first questions asked of him is "Is it a tewp or a yowe?"

But the horse provides most words. An entire horse is a *stallion*; a colt a *cowt*; a mare sometimes a *meear*; a foal often a *foil*; but a filly always a *filly.* The horse, like Northerners, has *lugs* and *wang-teeth* – "molars." To start him you shout *Hey!* and to stop him *Wey-ya!* You may be dealing with an unbroken horse called a *stag;* a *dog 'oss,* which is one that *tons orkerd* – "turns awkward; or a *jibber,* which is one that won't even start. But they know Yorkshire dialect. Shout *Wummit!* and see what happens.

As in Standard English, people are compared with animals. Only a few such names show affection (e.g. *duckie, lamb, owd dog*); most reveal the opposite (*ass, swine, bitch, cow,* etc). But Yorkshire revels in animal comparisons of its own. *Grasshopping* is following courters. *Monkey* applied to children means mischievous or cheeky ("Little monkeys!"), but with adults has a worse meaning (a malicious gossip will be called a "nasty monkey"). You can be "as fat as a mawk," i.e. maggot; "stink like a powcat" or "sweat like a brock"; "as fierce as a ratten"; "as wake (i.e. weak) as a kittlin"; "as wick as a scopprill" (squirrel); or "as green as a gezzlin." Mothers often reprimand their untidy children, "Yer little ullet" (i.e. owlet), or more carefully before strangers *hullet*, talking *bay-winder-like.*

STATUS SYMBOLS

YORKSHIRE FOLK are pleasantly ambitious, and it is only human to feel "wun up on t'next dooar Joneses" if you've got a *fur coit*, two cars or a colour *telly*, or just flown back for Majorca, and they haven't. If you have nothing to boast about, it's best to say *nowt* and let them make wild guesses. The first prize at a mid-Yorkshire workingmen's club was alleged to be one week at a certain resort and the second prize two weeks there. That was where holidaymakers were promised reductions if they made their own beds – and given hammer and nails. Well, that is just the sort of thing to keep very quiet about.

Status symbols change. In the terraced house districts an important one used to be the *sheffoneer*. The more elaborate its columns, mirrors, etc., the higher was its status; its cherished, highly polished surface was usually protected by lace mats on which stood a bewildering collection of *whim-whams* in cheap pot and glass, photos, sea-shells, artificial flowers and any other objects which would reflect credit on the household. The *cornish* above the parlour fireplace would carry the same type of decoration.

The parlour itself with its comfortable armchairs was most important. It might have an aspidistra and would if at all possible be equipped so that the family could say "Ahr Martha's larnin' t'pianer". Later, before turning into the modern *lounge*, it became *t'sittin'-room, t'best room,* or *t'front room*. Some parts of Yorkshire still call it just t'room, as if it is the only one they have worth calling a room.

Undignified *petties* or *privies* have given way to elaborate loos; antiquated yard-brushes, brooms and *besoms* to hoovers, etc; *ass-oils, bellowses, draw tins* and old-fashioned fireplaces to the luxuries of central heating. Yet old traditions and names do not easily die, and examples are most noticeable in the relaxed area of the home. For example, in the modern Fridge Age with its electric mixers, microwaves, jacuzzis etc., we might think the word *posser* has died with the possers themselves; but doubtless somewhere in Yorkshire at this moment a woman who has loaded and switched on *t'lektric* for her automatic washing machine is telling a neighbour, "Ah've just put t'clooas in ter poss."

However, some of the new gadgets can be a handicap. "Ah telled thee tha shouldn't 've weshed t'parrot i'Persil," argued one Tyke. "It weren't Persil 'at killed 'im," protested his neighbour, "it were t'spin-draher." Use all status symbols with descretion, please – a white rose soon gets mucky down the pit and a flat 'at looks out of place in church. Choose them sensibly – if you are watching Leeds, *flat 'at* and *muffler*; if fishing, sou'-wester and *ganzy*; if farming, *owd topcoit* and *yorkies* to keep your *britches'* legs up.

But we can't do much for those blind folk who can't see marks of success. "Come on," said an elderly Leeds lady, tugging at the sleeve of her son whom the estate agent was showing round a beautiful Bramhope residence, "come on, it's nobbut second-hand."

Speech is an odd thing, status-wise. In Yorkshire, good solid working-class children say *mam, mamma* or *mammy*, lower middle-class *mother*, and upper crust middle-class *mama*. *Mummy* seems to be more recent, possibly from the works of Enid Blyton. Adults also have different speech levels, but they must remember that any *lah-de-dah* effects can be spoilt by unsuitable vocabulary.

All Yorkshire dealect is struggling for higher status. Scottish and Irish are respected as national languages and even a South-Western burr is thought pleasant, whereas Southerners look down on our Northern lingo. Surely this is wrong. Give our dialect the honour it deserves.

"T'PAPERS, TELLY AND WIRELESS"

SOME OF the Tyke's greatest friends are his local papers. What need of *The Times* or the sensational national ones when good solid news is regularly supplied by worthy local papers with resounding, comforting names like Bradford's *Telegraph & Argus* or Huddersfield's *Daily Examiner*? For quick news, the Halifax *Evening Courier* series, for example, should match all rivals, and Sheffield's *Star* should enlighten any of the mind's dark corners.

No national papers can hold a candle to Yorkshire's local press. From the mighty *Yorkshire Post* in the west, to Scarborough's *Evening News* in the east, these successful papers meet a great need. Besides giving enough outside news, they act as local watchdogs. Whether parks are being vandalised or a local piggery is making a *tidy bloomin' stink,* they provide a platform for debate and complaint. Through their ads, they show what is available; and they bind together Yorkshire communities.

To find what Mrs. Thompson wore at her lass's wedding or who provided the garden party teas, seach your local paper. If Father Time is weighing you down, you can be comforted with news of local *old stagers* who generally seem to be enjoying good health and an active life. If they can last out cheerfully, so can you. Sometimes their pages reveal vivid social changes ("In them days I worked 55 hours a week for 6d an hour"). Furthermore they celebrate the real heroes – not "pop stars" and sex symbols, but responsible local stalwarts who quietly work to benefit their communities.

Admittedly there remain unfortunate pockets of resistance to *reeadin'*. In one small Yorkshire town the mayor's library was badly burned. Both books were damaged and he hadn't finished colouring one.

As for the other mass media, there is no need for suspicion, like the old lady who, *fleyed* ("afraid") the announcer would see her, used to drape a towel over her *telly* when she was getting *weshed*. Radio, B.B.C.'s *Look North* and Yorkshire T.V. news programmes certainly cover local events, characters and controversies very well, but of course we hear the full dialect only intermittently. If we heard it all the time, programmes might come over like this: Eigh up! Earken this!

Works Noos: Yon Yorksher mahners is laikin' again whahl they've getten a bit moor brass ... But t'mills is lookin' up. Umpteen ooarders is comin' in an' t'weyvers is skitterin' abaht rahnd t'looms lahk scawded cocks.

Ollerdy Noos: Off Fahla, some fooaks spa-in' ("on a pleasure trip") ver' near got drahnded. They'd getten a good lot o' mops ("small codlings") an' shremps when there came a jowl ("sea-swell") an' a blash ("sudden squall"). There were a reight slang-bang ("tangle of fishing lines"), t'booat started lekkin' an' they only just med it to t'Kye ("Bridlington Quay").

Forrin Noos: Wolves drew wi t'Toffees i't'Cup nowt-nowt ... T'rugby league fahnal will still be at Wembley ... Them stayin' ovver Kesmas ("Christmas") wi' relations i'Newcastle mun apply for visas.

For t'Missus: Tax is dahn on peggies, piggins, crackets, voiders an' posnets[1]. Dooan't cale ("queue-jump"), there's plenty on 'em, an' it'll be as easy as owt to stayven ("order") 'em whahl t'back-end ("autumn").

([1] Respectively sticks for tuning clothes in the wash-tub, lading cans, stools, clothes baskets and saucepans).

PART 2
THE YORKSHIREMAN'S DICTIONARY

OVER FORTY years ago I was introduced to a most knowl-
edgeable and well-known Tyke who amongst other labours
was enthusiastically compiling a Yorkshire dictionary.
Unfortunately he died with the work incomplete and all these
years we have had to struggle without such an essential aid.
Certainly one is badly needed for, if someone grumbles that
he is **clemmed, flummoxed, jiggered**, **starved** or **reyt nesh**,
you want to know just what is meant. If he says to you,
"Thoo gert, gallock-'anded, gaumless gawk," or "Get thi lug-
'oils cleyned aht," it is helpful to know whether this is high
praise, neutral comment or something else.

This dictionary has been produced from long residence and
travel round Yorkshire, where, for example, I was the field-
worker for the authoritative Leeds University *Survey of
English Dialects* under Professor Harold Orton, supplemented
by recent expeditions to check, update and add to material.
Most grateful thanks are due to the English Language depart-
ments of Leeds and Sheffield Universities, members of the
Yorkshire Dialect Society and very many people up and down
the shire who have willingly answered questions and/or provided the racy Yorkshire talk from which the Dictionary has
been made.

Yorkshire, being easily England's largest county, has a
wonderful store of special words, and the task of trying to
sort out the most typical has been fascinating. Most are root-
ed centuries deep in the past; for in Anglo-Saxon times the
region belonged to Northumbria, which was not just
Northumberland but, as the name suggests, almost all the
land in England north of the Humber east of the Pennines and
probably the Ribble to the west. It spoke Northumbrian, the
branch of Old English which has yielded our modern
Northern dialects.

Yorkshire is the land of Tykes. Anyone born there is one,
so that all those whose work, retirement or love life has
forced them to stray outside its borders are still thankfully
Tykes. But the county is always ready to accept suitable
recruits. Any **incomer** such as lapsed **Lanky** from the wrong

side of the Pennines, a Cockney **sparrer** or a **Brummager**, is welcome, in the minds of most generous-hearted Tykes, to trial membership and eventually, if proved keen enough, to full status.

This guide is intended for dyed-in-the-wool natives, new settlers and, not least, visitors bemused by "Yorkshire as it's spokken". Of course, the fact that a word like **mardy** or **muckworm** appears in our list does not necessarily deny it to other counties – Tykes are not so bigoted. But it does mean that it is alive, sometimes most vigourously alive, in the Ridings.

A common Yorkshire grumble about most dictionaries is that their stories are too short. Another complaint, voiced for instance by a Wakefield miner visiting the Tate gallery, was "T'pictures are aw reet but there's nooa jokes under 'em." We use words with a sprinkling of pictures, so will have to do our best.

A third problem for this dictionary, where space is limited, has been to show representative local pronunciations. In very general terms, the main division in pronouncing words lies between the predominantly industrial West Riding and the mainly agricultural North and East Ridings, so that for instance, West Riding **ooam** ("home") equals North and East Riding **yam, eeam**, etc., whilst West Riding **coil** ("coal"), **foil** ("foal") and **'oil** ("hole") stand respectively for **cooal, fooal,** and **'ooal** elsewhere in the county. However, Yorkshire is dialectally far more varied, in words and how to say them. Thus we can merely give you here plenty of sample Yorkshirisms, knowing that your good sense will show you which are used and just how in your immediate part of the White Rose county. Every dictionary at once needs a supplement, which often takes years and years to gather, but luckily you can supplement yours right now and in a most natural and interesting way just by listening to other Tykes.

So here at last is your vital language aid. Slip it handily into your pocket or guard it zealously for reference on your bookshelf. Study it, criticise it, add to it. Like Yorkshire's living language, a medium for joy, sorrow, anger, love and all other emotions, it is completely at your service.

A

aboon. above.
"It's a bit aboon me." – It's a bit too hard for me.

addle. earn.
"E addles lots o'brass." – He earns plenty of money.

afooar. before.
"E'll come afooar neet." – He'll come before night.

agate. started, going.
"Let's gang agate." – Let's get started.

ageean. again.
"Nah an'ageean." – Now and again.

'agworm. adder.
"Yon 'agworm'll bite." – That adder will bite.

'ahs, 'oos, etc. house.
"'Ere's ahr 'ahs." – Here's our house.

'ahsumivver. however.
"Ahsumivver, Ah manished." – However, I managed.

'aigs. haws.
"Aigs grows on a 'aig-tree." – Haws grow on a hawthorn bush.

alicker. (from ale + French aigre "sour"). vinegar.
"Fotch a pint of alicker." – Fetch a pint of vinegar.

allock. dawdle.
"They're allockin' abaht." – They're dawdling about.

ammot. am not.
"I ammot walkin' no farther." – I am walking no farther.

an' aw. also.
"Their lass (daughter) is clever an' bonny an' aw (pretty too)."

anent. next to.
"I sat me dahn anent 'im." – I sat down next to him.

'angers. hinges.
"This dooar needs noo 'angers." – This door needs new hinges.

ankled up. entangled.
"T'kite's gitten (has become) 'ankled up real bcad (very badly)."

apiece. each.
"Two bob (shillings) apiece."

'appen. perhaps.
"'Appen Ah sal (I shall) an 'appen Ah sahn't (I shan't)."

'appin. Wrapping, cover.
"We've neea (no) 'appin on t'bed."

April noddy. April fool.
"Catched tha! April noddy." – Caught you! April fool.

arse-end. bottom.
"Arse-end o' t'shaffs." – Bottoms of the sheaves.

arse-pocket. back trouser pocket.
"T'keigh (key)'s i' mi arse-pocket."

Arve! Turn left! (call to horses).
"She'll nawther gee (neither go right) nor arve." (Said of a stubborn woman.)

ask. newt.
"We seed asks i' t'pond." – We saw newts in the pond.

assle- pin. linch-pin.
"T'assle-pin's come oot." – The linch-pin has come out.

ass-middin. ash heap.
"She'll stop natterin' when t'ship lands on t'ass-middin." – She'll never stop arguing.

ass-nook. space beneath fire-grate.
"A mahs run aht (mouse ran out) o' t'ass-nook."

asteed. instead.
"E wore a dicky asteed of a shirt."

at. who(m), which, that.
"Fowk at's poor." (people who are poor); "nowt at Ah knows on." (nothing that I know about.)

at-after. afterwards.
"Plooin' fost, sowin' at-after." – Ploughing first, sowing afterwards.

attercrop. spider.
"Sweep dahn yon attercrop-web." – Sweep down that spider's web.

'attock. hattock, shock of 10

sheaves.

"A good wind'll blow yon (those) 'attocks o'er."

atween. between.

"Atween them two." – Between those two.

avver-bread. oatcake.

"Reyk a bit o'avver-bread off t'fleyk, wilta?" – Reach a bit of oatcake off the oatcake frame (under farmhouse ceiling), will you?

'awf. half.

"Awf-a-crahn." – Half-a-crown.

awlus. always.

"E awlus comes to t'chapel latt (late)."

ax. ask.

"Ah nivver axed 'im." – I never asked him.

axle-teeth. molars.

"Mi axle-teeth do warch (ache)."

aye. yes.

"Aye, we've getten (got) it."

B

babby. baby.

"T'babby's skrikin' (screeching)."

back-end. autumn.

"This back-end's nobbut dowly (only dull)."

back'ards-rooad. backwards.

"Brake, tha nit (you fool)! T'car's runnin' back'ards-rooad."

backside. politer than arse.

"Ah'll pawse thi backside." – I'll kick your posterior.

backstan. bake-stone (e.g. for oatcakes).

"As nimble as a cat on a 'eeat (hot) back-stan".

bahn. going.

(from Old Norse b inn "prepared").

"Ah'm bahn 'ooam." – I'm going home.

baht. without.

"On Ilkla' Moor baht 'at."

bairn. child.

"Daddy's bairn." – A child like its father.

bait + bitin'-on. snack.

"We's want mooar bait nor this." – We shall want a bigger snack than this.

balks. hay-loft.

"Whitewesh t'balks." – Whitewash the hay-loft.

band. string.

"Nut woth a band's end." – Not worth the end of a piece of string.

bang. beat.

"Bang is beeans." – Beat his bones. Also: "Livin' bang + Livin' Allelujah." – Living "in sin" as man and wife.

bant. Strength, courage. See also spunk.

"E's got some bant on 'im." – He has plenty of courage.

barkum. horse-collar.

"They welted (tipped) t'cart ower an' brak (broke) t'barkum."

barm. yeast.

"Fotch a few pennorth (pennyworth) o' barm."

bate. reduce in price.

"Thou mun bate summat." – You must reduce your price to some extent.

beal + blart. bellow.

"A bealin' cah sooin forgets its cauf." – A bellowing cow soon forgets its calf.

beck. stream.

"Weshed doon t'beck." – Washed down the stream.

beeak. bake.

"Beeaked a ceeak." – baked a cake.

beeath + booath. both.

"Beeath on us." – both of us.

beeas. cows.

"'Osses an' beeas." – horses and cows.

beet. make or repair nets.

"They're beetin' their nets bi t'cobles (sharp-bowed keel-less fishing boats

as at Filey)."

belk. belch.
"Tha belks when tha's full an' when tha's empty."

bellowses (double plural). bellows.
"There's neea (no) wind left i' t'bellowses."

belly-button. navel.
"Clobber (hit) 'im i't'belly button."

belly-wark. stomach-ache.
"Uddled (hunched) up wi' t'belly-wark."

beltikite. good-for-nothing.
"E's nobbut (only) a beltikite."

bensel. thrash.
"Ah'll bensel yer 'ide." – I'll thrash your hide.

bent. rough grass.
"Mossy peeats amang t'bent." – Mossy peat among the rough grass.

bezzle. eat greedily.
"E's bezzlin' ageean (again)."

biddy. louse.
"As lish (agile) as a biddy."

black-bum + bummel-kite. blackberry.
"Eyt them black-bums." – Eat those blackberries.

black-leead. black-lead.
"Ossett's wheer (where) they used to black-leead t'tramlines."

blaeberries. bilberries.
"There's a gay two or three (quite a few) blaeberries."

blash. sudden squall.
"It come a gret blash o' rain" – There came a great rain-squall.

bleb + plish-'ole (e.g. in Dentdale). blister.
"A bleb o' mi'eel (on my heel)."

bleg. gather blackberries.
"Childer (children) like to go bleggin'."

blether. talk nonsense.
"What arta (are you) bletherin' abaht (about)?"

blether-'eead. empty-headed fool.
"You're a set o'blether-'eeads."

blether-lugs + bletherskite. tell-tale, gossip.
"'Od thi tung, blether-lugs!" – Hold dour tongue, tell-tale!
"shoo's an awfu' bletherskite." – She's an awful gossip.

blinnd pap/tit. teat giving no milk. See also deeaf pap/tit.
"This 'ere coo (this cow) ez a blinnd tit."

blinnders. blinkers.
"Lift that' 'oss's (horse's) blinnders off."

blob. bubble.
"T'pool's all ower blobs." – The pool's filled with bubbles.

blodder. cry out.
"Tooithwark meks me blodder." – Toothache makes me cry out.

Bloody + bloody-ally. marble streaked with red.
"Let's lake wi' (play with) bloodies."

bobby-'oil. police station.
"They're tekkin 'im (taking him) to t'bobby-'oil."

bog-bellied. corpulent.
"Tha's getten reyt bog-bellied." – You've become exceedingly fat.

boggard. ghost; goblin.
"Flayed wi' boggards." – Frightened by ghosts.

boke. retch.
"Ah fair boked (I really retched) at it."
booit. boot.
"Dusta (do you) like mi tan booits?"

bool. curved handle.
"T'bool o' this bucket's mighty cowd (very cold)."

boose. cow-stall.
"There's plenty o' booses i' t'mistle (old-fashioned cow-house)."

boskin. upright between cow-stalls.
"Tee yon 'eifer up to t'boskin." – tie that heifer to the upright. See also

skell-boose.

brak. broke.
"It brak aw to smash." – It broke completely.

Brant. steep.
"T'trod (the path)'s as brant as a 'oos (house)-side."

brass. money.
"E stinks o'brass." – i.e. He has too much money.

brassock. charlock.
"Sis (Cicely) is pooin' (pulling) brassocks."

brat. coarse apron (e.g. a cobbler's).
"Thy greeasy brat." – Your greasy apron.

bray. beat.
"Get thee yam or Ah'll bray thee." – Get home or I'll beat you.

breeten up. brighten.
"It's breetnin' up." – The weather is brightening.

bribe. damaged length of cloth.
"E's gin (he has given) me a bribe."

brig. bridge.
"Yebden Brig." – Hebden Bridge.

brim. be on heat.
"T'soo's brimmin'." – The sow is on heat.

britches. trousers.
"T' missus weears t'britches as weel as t'bloomers." – My wife wears the breeches as well as the bloomers, i.e. she is the boss.

brock. badger.
"This place stinks woss nor (worse than) a brock."

brokken. broken.
"She'd neea beeans (no bones) brokken."

browis. oatcake dipped in fat, gravy, etc.
"A mess (meal) o'nettle podish (porridge) an' browis."

bruff. health-looking.
"Bruff an' lish (active)."

brussen. burst.
"That theer boil's brussen." – that boil has burst.

brussen-guts. glutton.
"Stop bezzlin' (eating greedily), brussen-guts!"

bucky. strong and resistant, of dough.
"This dough's ower (too) bucky."

buffle-'eead. stupid fellow.
"They've sent us a buffle-'eead."

bug. delighted.
"As bug as a lad wi' a noo casey (new case-ball)."

bull-'eeads. tadpoles.
"T'pond's full o' bull-'eeads."
bull-front, bull-forred (-forehead),

bull-feeace (-face). tussock.
"Cahs awlus leeave them bull-fronts." – Cows always leave those tussocks.

bullin'. on heat, of cows.
"Fotch (fetch) t'bull: she's a-bullin'."

bummel-kites. See blackbums.
blackberries.

Bunfire Neet. Bonfire Night.
"T'bairns (the children) love Bunfire Neet." See also Plot Neet.

butty. bread-and-butter sandwich.
Early ones were filled with brown sugar. A nasty trick, by men of course, was to make a wasp butty. "Ah do love sugar butties, jam butties an' traycle (treacle) butties."

buzzard. moth.
"As blinnd (blind) as a buzzard."

By gum! By God! Good gracious!
"By gum, it's thine." – By God, it's yours.

byre. old-fashioned cowhouse.
Compare mistle + shippon.
"E gans into t'byre." – He goes into the cowhouse.

C

cabal. noisy talk.
"What a cabal! Ah cornt 'ear missen

speyk (I can't hear myself speak)."

cack-'anded + caggy + ceggy.
left handed.
*"Thoo's a cack-'anded cuddy paw." –
You're left handed.*

cale. queue-jump.
*"Ey up! Tha's calin me." – Hey!
You're taking my place.*

calkers. clog-irons.
*"Keep thi gret (great) calkers off mah
feet."*

call. gossip.
*"She's awlus callin' aboot." – She's
always gossiping.*

caller. gossiper.
*"Ah's 'evin' neea callers." – I'm hav-
ing no gossipers.*

cannle. candle.
*"Ah corn't see bi cannle-leet." – I
can't see by candle-light.*

canny. well thought of (often com-
bined with larl).
*"A canny larl thing." – A pleasant lit-
tle thing.*

cap. surpass; surprise.
*"That caps (beats) t'lot on 'em";
"Ah'm fair capped at thi (astonished
at you)."*

cappil. patch (e.g. on a shoe).
"Pur (put) a cappil on."

carr. marshy land.
Carr Gate near Wakefield.

cart-arse + cart-'eck. rear of cart.
*"Stop, yer gawby (fool): t'cart-arse
'as tummled oot (tumbled out)."*

case-clock. grandfather clock.
*"Tha's bowt a champion (bought an
excellent) case-clock."*

catie-cornered. diagonally.
"Od (hold) that sack catie-cornered."

caumeril. pole on which a slaughtered pig is hung.
"As crooked as a caumeril."

causey. pavement.
*"Shoo come thrutchin' (She came
pushing) past us on t'causey."*

cawf-'eead. fool.

*"Gan on, thoo gret cawf-'eead!" –
Nonsense you great fool!*

cawf-licked. with hair sticking out
from the forehead.
*"E's roon-shoodert (round-shoul-
dered) an' cawf-licked."*

ceeads. cades, sheep-lice.
*"To kill ceeads, sheep mun (must)
be salved."*

chaff-'earted. cowardly.
*"Ev some guts (have some courage)
– tha's chaff-'earted."*

champion. excellent.
*"It were fair champion." – It was real-
ly excellent.*

chayamly. chamberlye, stale
urine.
*"Cah-muck an' chayamly meks a
pultiss better." – cow manure and
stale urine improve a poultice.*

checker-brat. checked linen over-
all, generally worn by wool
sorters.
*"Ast seed (have you seen) mi check-
er-brat?"*

cheggies. string of horse hest-
nuts.
"Let's lake (play) wi' cheggies."

chelp. talk loudly.
"Chelp! Chelp! Fro' mornin' till neet!"

chimley. chimney.
*"Sat i' t'chimley-nook." – Sitting in the
chimney-corner.*

chip-oil + chippy + fish-' oil. fish-
and-chip shop.
"T'chip-'oil's oppen (open)."

chitlins. pig's entrails.
"We'll start wi' t'chitlins."

choch. church.
*"T'owd wimmin (old women) does
love a choch weddin'."*

chomp. chew vigorously.
*"Dooan't chomp yon spice." – Don't
chew those sweets.*

chonce 'un. illegitimate child.
*"Tha knows (you know) 'e's a
chonce 'un."*

choose-'ow. in any case.
"Mester Smith'll preych next Sunda i' t'morn. Ah sal preych at neet, choose-'ow." – Mr. Smith will preach next Sunday morning. I shall preach in the evening, whatever happens.

choose-what. whatever.
"E wain't side wimmi (won't agree with me), choose-what I says."

chuff(ed). pleased.
"Tha's varry chuff sin tha gat that brass left." – You're very pleased since you were left that money.

chump, + prog (e.g. at Silsden). collect wood, etc. for Bonfire Night.
"Let's go chumpin'."

chunner. grumble.
"E's chunnered for lang aneeaf." – He's grumbled long enough.

clack. clatter.
"What art (are you) clackin' at, woman?"

clap-cowd. very cold.
"Kessmas Eve were clap-cowd." – Christmas Eve was very cold.

clart-'eead. fool.
"Nobbut (only) a clart-'eead'd want a dollop (lump) o' mud."

clarty. dirty.
"Wesh thi clarty 'ands." – Wash your dirty hands.

clay joss. clay tobacco-pipe.
"Ah've fun t'baccy (found the tobacco) for mi clay joss."

cleg. horse fly.
"E' stuck like a cleg."

clem. starve with hunger.
"Clemmed to deeath." – Desperately hungry.

cletch. clutch of eggs; family of children.
"E comes of a bad cletch (family)."

clever-clogs. conceited person.
"Yah, clever-clogs!" – Nonsense, 'big-head'!

climm. climb.

"Climm ower (climb over) t'stile."

cloamy. sticky.
"Traycle (treacle)'s cloamy."

clobber. strike.
"Ah'll clobber thi lug-oil (your ear-hole)."

clock. any kind of beetle.
"T'kitchen flooar (floor)'s full o'clocks."

clocker. broody hen.
"Yon clocker wain't lay." – That broody hen won't lay.

cloise. close, near; enclosed field.
"Cloise togither (close together); cooarn (corn)'s growin' i' t'close."

clomp. tread heavily.
"E comes (came) clompin' in ovver mi cleean flooar (clean floor)."

clout. dish-cloth.
"Fotch us (fetch med) a clout, Mary."

clouts. clothes.
"Ah doffed (took off) mi clouts."

cock-eyed. cross-eyed.
"Shoo were skennin' (she was squinting) at me, cock-eyed."

cock-stride. very short distance.
"It's nobbut (only) a cock-stride to t'pooast (post-) office."

cock-thropple. Adam's apple.
"Mi cock-thropple's sooar (sore)."

cockle. phlegm.
"Is cockle's full o'blood."

cod. See also swad. pod (of pea).
"Shill them pea-cods." – Shell those pea-pods.

codder. leader of a steelworks press-forging team.
"E's ahr codder". – He's our team-leader.

coddin'-time. British summer time.
"It stays leeter at neet (lighter in the evening) i' coddin'-time."

coil-'oil + coil-'ahs. cellar.
"We're reyt dahn i' t'coil-'oil." – We're right down in the cellar.

coit. coat.

"It's cowd baht (cold without) mi coit."
collop. chunk slice.
"A collop o'bacon."
come. on.
"come Setda (on Saturday) I'll be at Ellan Rooad (Elland Road)."
come. came.
"An' then thoo come (you came)."
comer-in. stranger.
"They're comers-in, they've nobbut bin i'Crayke thotty year (30 years)."
copper-'aws. poppies.
"Pick some copper-'aws from t'cloise (field)."
cornish. cornice.
"It's liggin' (lying) on t'cornish."
cottered. tangled.
"Comm thi lung 'air: it's cottered." – comb your long hair: it's tangled.
cow-clap. cow-dropping.
"Mind (beware) that cow-clap; she's as common as cow-claps."
cow-lady. ladybird.
"Ah've copt (I've caught) a cow-lady."
cowl-rake. ember-rake.
"Wheer's tha putten (where have you put) t'cowl-rake?"
cracket. stool.
"Sit thi doon (sit down) on this 'ere (this) cracket."
cracks. chaps on hands.
"Ah've getten some reet cracks." – I've got some bad chaps.
cranch. crunch.
"Cranchin' seea mony (so many) apples."
crazy booan. funny bone.
"Ouch! Ah've banged mi crazy booan."
cree. soften by boiling gently.
"Frummety an' rice wants weel creein' (need plenty of gentle boiling)."
crow. hard nasal muscus.
"See you drahver (that driver) at t'leets (traffic-lights) pickin' 'is crow?"
crowdy. oatmeal gruel.

"We mostlins (generally) 'ed crowdy for supper."
crozzled. shrivelled and over-cooked.
"Mi meeat (meat)'s crozzled."
crud. curdle.
"Milk at's crudded." – Milk that is curdled.
cuddy. donkey.
"As fond (foolish) as a cuddy."
cuddy-wifted. left-handed.
Also cuddy-fisted/-flipped/-pawed.
cushat. wood-pigeon.
"E's gan (gone) shootin' cushats i' t'bottom wood."
Cush-up! Come here! (call to cows).

D

daft. silly.
"As daft as a gooise (goose)."
dawkey. over-dressed.
"Oor lass is gettin' ower dawkey". – Our daughter is becoming too over-dressed.
daytalman. farm labourer (paid by the day).
"Ah warked theer (worked there) as a daytalman." See also Knockaboot, Tommy-out.
dazed. addled.
"T'eggs was (the eggs were) all dazed."
dee. die.
"Nobdy ivver dees wi' warkin' feet." – Nobody ever dies with working feet.
deead. dead; absolutely.
"Deead i't'middle." – Right in the middle.
deeaf. deaf.
"Deeaf as a stoop (post)."
deeaf pap/tit. teat not giving milk.
"She's deeaf on a pap." – One of the cow's teats can't work.
deg. sprinkle.

"Fotch a sup o'watter to deg thm cleeas wi'." – Fetch a little water to sprinkle those clothes.

delf. quarry.
"A stooan (stone) delf."

dick(y). louse.
"Let's cemm t'dickies out o' thi yed." – Let me comb the lice out of your head.

dike. hedge, ditch.
"Cut yon dike (hedge); sprawlin' i't'dike (ditch) bottom."

ditherums + dodders. tremors.
"E's getten t'ditherums." – He's got the tremors.

dobber. large marble.
"Thoo (you)'ll not win mi dobber"

docken. dock (the weed).
"T'garden's snided out (over-run) wi' dockens."

doddy. hornless cow.
"Dooan't be feared (don't be afraid) of a doddy."

doff. undress.
"Get thi doffed." – Get undressed.

dog-'ull. kennel.
"Ah's fettlin' (I'm repairing) t'dog-'ull."

dollop. lump.
"Grab this dollop o'dumplin'."

dolly-posh. left-handed.
See also cack-anded, cuddy-wifted.

don. put on.
"Don thi bonnet, bairn." – Put on your bonnet, child.

donnat. idler (literally do naught).
"Thou gormless (senseless) donnat!"

dooar-'oil. doorway.
"Stannin' (standing) i' t'dooar-'oil."

dosn't. durst not.
"Shoo dosn't gan ooam." – She durst not go home.

doughy. stupid.
"Tha's reyt (you're quite) doughy."

dowk. dive.
"Dowt under t'brig." – Dive under the bridge.

dowly. dull, miserable (of people or weather).
"It's a dowly day; Ah feels varry dowly baht'er (very miserable without her)."

doy. affectionate term for a child.
"Whooa's bin ooinin' tha, doy?" – Who's been distressing you, love?

dree. tedious.
"It's a dree job, cuttin' beeans (beans)."

druffen. drunk.
"Thoo druffen tyke." – You drunken Yorkshireman.

dummle 'eead. blockhead.
"Tha gert gormless (great sense-less) dummle 'eead!"

dunch. bump, shove.
"E gev (gave) me a dunch wi' 'is elber (with his elbow)."

dunnock. hedge-sparrow.
"As dark as a dunnock."

E

'eart-sluffened. heart-broken.
"Shoo looked fair 'eart-sluffened." – She looked quite heart-broken.

'eccups. hiccups.
"Ah've getten t'eccups." – I've got hiccups.

'eck. hay-rack.
"There's good sweet 'ay in t'eck."

eead, yed, etc. head.
"Frae eead to fooit." – From head to foot.

'eeaf. pasture-ground.
"Ton 'em oot onto t'eeaf." – Turn them out on to the heaf.

'eeam, 'ooam, yam. home.
"Ah's comin' yam." – I'm coming home.

eeasins. house-eaves.
"T'rain's drippin' off t'eeasins."

een. eyes.
"Ah've getten (I've got) two black een for feytin' (in fighting)."

'eft. accustom sheep to new pasture.
"Ah's 'eftin a scooar o'sheep."

Eigh up! Hello!; Look out!
"Eigh up theer! 'Ow do?" – Hello there. How are you; "Eigh up! (Look out!) There's a puddle-oil (puddle)."

'en coit + 'en-'oil, 'en-'ull, 'en-'ut. hen-house.
"Cleyn aht (clean out) t'en-coits."

entire. stallion.
"Yon (that)'s a good entire."

'errin'-gutted. thin, ill-nourished.
"She's 'errin'-gutted, t'same size all t'way up."

etten. eaten.
"Thi supper's etten." – Your supper's eaten.

ettle. intend.
"What's thoo ettlin' at (what do you intend) wi' that stick?"

eyt. eat.
"Ah can eyt owt." – I can eat anything.

eyvy-ceyvy. uncertain, wavering.
"That mill chimley (chimney) looks eyvy-ceyvy (about to fall)."

F

fain. very glad.
"Ah's fain to sithee." – I'm very glad to see you.

fair. local festival. See also feeast.
"Tawmdin (Todmorden) Fair Wipsa (Wibsey) Fair, Weeton (Market Weighton) Fair."

fair. quite.
"It's fair shameful."

fart. break wind. Besides politer let off + trump.
"Tha's farted."

fash. trouble, worry.
"Deean't thee fash thisell." – Don't worry.

favver. resemble.

"Thi favvers thi dad." – You resemble your father.

feeast. local festival or holiday. Compare fair.
"Gargrave Feeast, Gerston (Grassington) Feeast."

feckless. useless.
"It's feckless wark." – It's useless work.

feld. felloe (of wheel).
"They welted (tipped) t'cart ower an' brak (broke) two felks."

felted. confused.
"Ah's felted when Ah 'earken Geordies." – I'm confused when I listen to Tynesiders.

fern-tickles. freckles. See also sparrer-farts.
"Shoo 'es (she has) lots o' fern-tickles."

fettle. prepare; mend.
"Frida's fettlin' day." – Friday's cleaning day.

feyt. fight.
"Oor dogs is feytin'." – Our dogs are fighting.

finnd. find.
"It's easier to finnd a fault nor to loise wun (than to lose one)."

fire-point. poker.
"Mi legs 'ave swelled (swollen) as thick as fire-points."

fizz-gig. gossip.
"Sike an owd fizz-gig." – Such an old gossip.

flake. rack fixed to ceiling for drying oatcakes.
"Lay 'em on t'flake."

flay (from Old Norse fleygja). frighten.
"Flayed to tek a missus." – Frightened to take a wife.

flay-crow. scarecrow.
"Flackerin' (flapping) about like flay-crows."

fleeak. hurdle.
"T'shepherd's moved them theer

fleeaks (those hurdles)."

fleear + flooar. floor.
"T'babby (baby)'s crawlin' ovver t'fleear."

fleet. skim milk.
"T'milk wants fleeting."

fleighsome. frightening.
"It's a fleighsome spot at neet." – It's a frightening place at night.

flibberty-gibbet. flighty or eccentric person.
"Shoo (she)'s a proper (real) flibberty-gibbet."

flick. flitch of bacon.
"Cut some collops (lumps) off yon (that) flick."

fligged. fledged.
"Them brids is fligged." – Those birds are fledged.

flipe. rim or peak of bonnet or cap.
"Touch thi flipe to t'squire."

flummoxed. bewildered.
"I were fair flummoxed." – I was utterly bewildered.

flunter. order.
"Thy loom is badly out o'flunter."

fodderem. passage along head of stalls in old cowhouse.
"T'ay-fork's i't'fodderem." – The hay fork's in the passage.

fog. second crop of grass.
"It'll aw mak (all make) good fog."

foil + fooal. foal.
"Yon mare's just lost 'er foil."

foisty. fusty.
"As foisty as an owd choch (old church)."

fond. foolish(ly).
"Deean't talk seea fond." – Don't talk so foolishly.

fooil + feeal. fool.
"Tha gert fooil, tha!" – You great fool!

fooit. foot.
"Stick yer fooit dahn (your foot down) on t'pedal."

fooitbaw. football.

for all. although.
"E sups (drinks) lots o'whisky, for all it's so dear."

forkin'-robin. earwig. Compare jinny-spinner, twitch-bell.
"There's a vast deal (great number) o' forkin'-robins."

forty-leg. centipede.
"Yon's anudder (that's another) forty-leg."

fost. first.
"My marrers (marrows) won fost prize."

fotch. fetch.
"Fotch them yeller cottans (those yellow curtains)."

fotty. forty.
"Fotty yer sin." – Forty years ago.

foul. ugly.
"As foul as a pot mule."

fowk(s). people.
"Fowks'll say owt." – People will say anything.

frame. show promise.
"Ah think 'e frames middlin' (he's doing fairly well)."

frap. behave ill-temperedly.
"What's Lizzy (Elizabeth) bin frappin' abaht?"

fratch. argument: argue.
"They're 'evin a regular good fratch (tremendous argument); fratchin' like cats."

freetened. frightened.
"E's nivver freetened." – He's never frightened.

fresh-fly. bluebottle.
"That fish is wick wi' (alive with) – fresh-flies."

froff. light, spongy.
"This ooak beeam (oak beam)'s froff."

frummety. dish of "hulled" wheat boiled in milk.
"Ow's frummety comin on?"

fummart. polecat.
"Them owd clooas (those old clothes) stink like a fummart."
fun. found.
"T'matches is fun." – The matches are found.
fuzzock. donkey, ass.
"As drunk as a fuzzock."

G

gallock-'anded. left-handed. See also cack-'anded, cuddy-wifted.
"E's a dab 'and at wark (an expert at work), if (even if) 'e is gallock-'anded."
gallowses (double plural). men's braces.
"Ah've brokken (broken) mi gallowses wi'bendin'."
gammy. lame, injured.
"Mind mi gammy fooit." – Beware my injured foot.
gapin'. yawning.
"Powfagged (exhausted) an' gapin'."
gapway. gateway.
"Aside t'gapway." – Beside the gateway.
garth. small piece of enclosed ground.
"T'owd (the old) farmer catched 'im in 'is apple-garth (orchard)."
gasbag. gossip.
"T'missus is a reyt gasbag." – My wife is a real gossip.
gate. way, path.
"Briggate i' (in) Leeds; a fooitgate (footpath) ger aht 'o t'gate (get out of the way)."
gaum. notice.
"Ah nivver gaumed 'im." – I never noticed him.
gaumless. foolish.
"As gaumless as a suckin' duck."
gavlock. crowbar.
"Wi mi gavlock ovver mi shooder." –

With my crowbar over my shoulder.
gawby. fool.
"Morley Gawbies; Wipsa (Wibsey) Gawbies" – Standard nicknames for the unfortunate natives of these places.
gawk. core of boil; fool.
"Ah corn't git t'gawk oot (I can't get the core out); thoo daft gawk (you silly fool)."
gawp. gape.
"Telly-gawpin'." – Gaping at television.
gay. very.
"Ah's gay pleeased to sethee." – I'm very pleased to see you.
gebby. loquacious
"A gebby woman should shut 'er gob (mouth)."
Gee! Turn right! (call to horses).
"Gee then! Gee a bit!"
gegged. thirsty.
"Ah's terble gegged." – I'm very thirsty.
getten. got.
"We've getten into t'wrang cooach (wrong coach)."
gilt (from Old Norse gylta). Young sow.
"That gilt's fattenin' up weel (well)."
gimmer. female sheep 1-2 years old or between 1st and 2nd shearings.
"'E selled me four owd gimmers." – He sold me four old gimmers.
gin. given.
"E's gin us nowt." – He's given me nothing.
ginnel + gennel. alleyway. See also snicket.
"Reyt up yon ginnel." – Righty up that alleyway.
gip. retch.
"It gives me gip." – It makes me retch.
gippy. starling. Compare shepster.
"Gippies wants shootin'." – Starlings

Giss! Giss! Come here! (call to pigs).

gizzened. satiated.
"Ah corn't eyt nooa mooar: ah's gizzened." – I can eat no more: I'm full.

glass-alleys. glass marbles.
"Len' us them (lend me those) glass-alleys."

glazner. severe frost that glazes.
"There'll be a glazner toneet (tonight)."

glishy. glittering (of the sky).
"It'll rain afooar neet (before night), it's seea (so) glishy."

gloppened. astounded.
"Ah were parfitly gloppened." – I was quite astounded.

goaf. space in mine from which coal has been extracted.
"Chuck it i' t'goaf." – throw it into the cavity.

gob(bler). mouth.
"She'd a gob like a backus (bake-house) oven; oppen (open) thi gobbler."

gob-a-tosh. person with prominent teeth.
"Ast sin yon (have you seen that) gob-a-tosh?"

gob-slotch. greedy person.
"Neea (no) wonder 'e's bog-bellied (corpulent), 'e's a gob-slotch."

gobsmacked. dumbfounded.
"Shoo were fair gobsmacked." – She was quite dumbfounded.

Gogsies! warning shout that marbles may be snatched.
"Gogsies! Big lads is comin'." – Marbles! Big boys are coming.

gollop. gulp.
"E' gollops 'is meyt." – He gulps his food.

Golly. Unfledged bird.
"a bare-golly nest".

gomerill. blockhead.
"Tha gomerill!"

goodies. sweets. See also spice.
"A 'ayporth (halfpenny-worth) o' goodies."

goois + geeas. goose.
"I'se aw (I'm all) goois-skin." – i.e. I'm shivering all over.

goose-gog. gooseberry.
"Them's reyt fine goose-gogs." – those are very fine gooseberries.

gowk. cuckoo; simpleton.
"As lazy as a gowk (cuckoo)"; "Any gowk (fool) should knaw not to sit 'issen dahn (sit down) on a pissimire (ant-) 'ill."

goyt. channel, mill-steam.
"It's agin t'goyt." – It's next to the mill-stream.

gradely. good, fine.
"A varra gradely body." – A very fine person.

grain. prong.
"T'grain o' t'muck-fork's bent bad." – The digging-fork prong is badly bent.

grease-horn. flatterer.
"Tha's nobbut a greasehorn." – You're only a flatterer.

greck. weakling of pig-litter; puny child.
"Johnny's t'greck of ahr family."

gripe. garden-fork.
"Tak t'gripe til it." – Take the garden-fork to it.

grob. dig. poke.
"Grob oot them dreeans." – Poke out those drains.

groin. snout.
"T'bull 'es a ring in its groin."

groop. drain in a cow-stall.
"Cow-muck (cow-manure) falls into t'groop."

grummle-guts. discontented person.
"'E's a regular (very great) grummle-guts."

grund. ground.
"Liggin' on t'grund." – Lying on the

ground.

gruns. dregs in tea-cup.
"Leeave t'gruns." – Leave the dregs.

gully. large knife.
"Chop it wi' t'gulley."

gumption. commonsense.
"E wants mooar gumption." – He needs more commonsense.

guts. stomach; fillings of a dry-stone wall.
"All gob an' guts (of greedy children); shove in plenty o' guts (fillings)."

guttle. drink greedily.
"Dooan't guttle sooa." – Don't drink so greedily.

I

ice-shockle. icicle.
"Lang ice-shockles danglin' doon." – Long icicles hanging down.

idleback. loose piece of skin near fingernail. Compare stepmother.

'ig. fit of temper.
"She flounced off in a mad 'ig."

'ilt. handle of spade.
"T'ilt's brokken." – The handle's broken.

inby. towards the coal face.
"T'colliers (miners) 'ave gone ti wark (work) inby."

'ingins + jemmers. hinges.
"T'dooar (the door)'s droppin' off its 'ingins."

ings. low-lying fertile land near a river. Compare 'olms.
"T'watter's gitten ower t'inges (double plural)" – The water has got over the ings.

'ipe. butt, gore.
"Gotten 'iped wi' (was gored by) that nasty bull."

'ippin. baby's nappy.
"Get this 'ippins off." – i.e. act like an adult.

Irish daisy. dandelion.

The Yorkshire system is to blame anything peculiar or unwanted on another part of the world. Compare Manchester sunshine (drizzle), Newcastle 'ospitality (too much of it), Brummagem screwdriver (hammer), to welsh, Dutch treat, etc.

ivvery. every.
"Ivvery wik." – Every week.

J

Jack Lob + Owd Nick. the Devil.
"Ah seed (I saw) Jack Lob i' t'chochyard (churchyard)."

jam-pot meyt. meatless meal (scornful term).
"Jam-pot meyt an' maggie (margarine)." – dogs dinner.

jart. beat.
"Jart that bairn's bum (child's bottom)."

jatter. to make vibrate.
"T'noise fra yon disco jattered mi yed." – The noise from that disco shook my head.

jawm. door post.
"Ageean t'dooar-jawm." – Next to the door-post.

jay-legged. knock-kneed.
"Yon weyver (that weaver) walks jay-legged."

jibber. horse that refuses to start.
"Jibbers is neea good." – Jibbers are no use.

Jiggered + pow-fagged. exhausted.
"Ah'm fair jiggered up." – I'm quite exhausted.

jinny-spinner. earwig. Compare forkin'-robin, twitch-bell.
"We're run ovver (overrun) wi' jinny-spinners."

jock. food.
"Ah've etten mi jock." – I've eaten my food.

joskin. farm labourer (jocular

term).

"A country joskin."

jotherum. quaking mass.

"Talk aboot a jotherum at t'dance!"

jowl. knock.

"Ah'll jowl their 'eeads togither (heads together)."

jubber. talk idiotically.

"Gie ower thi jubberin'." – Stop talking nonsense.

K

keck. tip.

"Keck up t'cart a larl bit." – Tip the cart a little.

Keckers. steps, e.g. to a bedroom.

"Mind (watch) them two keckers."

keck-stick. cart's tipping-bar.

"Git od (get hold) o' t'keck-stick."

keggly. unsteady.

"Yon stack's keggly."

kelt. money.

"Ony kelt, Bill?" – Have you any money, Bill?

kelter. rubbish.

"Nowt but aad kelter." – Nothing but old rubbish.

keslop. rennet.

"As teeaf (tough) as keslop."

Kessmas. Christmas.

"Aw t'bairns'll come wom at Kessmas." – All my children will come home at Christmas.

ket. offal.

"E stinks like owd (old) ket."

kindlin'. firewood.

"This 'ere (this) kindlin's damp."

kist. chest.

"A kist o' drawers."

kittle. bring forth kittens.

"Ahr cat's kittled ageean (again)."

kittle. delicate.

"As kittle as a moose (mouse)-trap."

kittlin. kitten.

"As wake (weak) as a kittlin."

knackers. the privates. (Compare Icelandic hnakkur "a scrape").

"Tak 'is knackers off: that'll queten 'im (of unruly horse)."

knep. bite playfully.

"Tweea 'osses kneppin' yan anudder." – Two horses playfully biting each other.

kneyd. knead.

"Kneyd t'duff noo." – Knead the dough now.

knockaboot. farm labourer. Compare daytalman, Tommy-owt.

"E's nobbut (only) a knockaboot".

knurr an' spell. game with wooden ball or hard knot of wood.

"Let's lake (play) at knurr an' spell."

kysty. fastidious.

"Shoo's turble kysty." – She's very fastidious.

-la. lea, pasture, in place-names.

E.g. Bairnsla (Barnsley), Emsla (Helmsley), Ilka (Ilkley), Otla (Otley), Shipla (Shipley), Stowsla (Stokesley).

lait. seek.

"'E's laiting' bod-nesses." – He's looking for birds' nests.

lake, laik. (from Old Norse Leika). play; be unemployed.

"Let's lake (play) at tig (touch); they're lakin' tally (playing truant); I've no brass (money) – I wor lakin' (was unemployed) all last month."

laky. playground.

"Er teycher (teacher) 's i' t'laky."

lap. wrap.

"Lap a clout (wrap a cloth) round it."

larl + lahtle. little.

"A larl canny box; a lahtle bit." – A nice little box; a little bit.

lathe. cow-house plus barn.

"Aback o' (behind) t'lathe."

latt. late.

"Ah'll be latt for schooil (school)."

learn (as in Middle English, e.g. in

The Ormulum). teach.
"E nivver learnt me owt." – He never taught me anything.
lee. lie, untruth.
"Ah corn't (can't) tell a lee."
leeaf. inner layer of fat round a pig's kidneys.
"It's getten a rare (good) leeaf on it."
leet. light.
"Leet t'fire; as clear as dayleet."
let off. break wind. See also fart, trump.
"Tha's letten off ageean." – You've broken wind again.
ley. scythe.
"Gan an' maw wi' yon ley." – Go to mow with that scythe.
lickerish. liquorice. Compare ending of cornish (cornice).
"Giz (give me) a lickerish awsooart (all-sort)."
lief. rather.
"Ah'd as lief stop." – I would rather stop.
lig. lie; lay.
"Sha ligs doon ivvery day (she lies down every day; lig (lay) that 'edge."
-like. can be almost meaningless space-filler.
"Mi fooit's aw swelled-like." – My foot is all swollen.
likeness. photograph.
"Tak 'is likeness quick." – Take his photograph quickly.
limmers. cart-shafts.
"Put t'oss i' t'limmers." – Put the horse in the shafts.
ling. heather.
"Ilkla (Ilkley) Moor's covered wi' ling."
lish. agile.
"A lish young un." – An agile young one.
lisk. groin.
"Ah've walked while (until) mi lisk's sair (sore)."
lithen. thicken.
"Lithen that broth, wilta (will you)?"

lobcock. clumsy idle fellow.
"Thoo 'are – brained (stupid) lobcock!"
lob-coddied + cross lonked. lopsided.
"That theer picture's lob-coddied." – That picture's lop-sided.
lob-loll. odd-job man.
"Ah knaws a lob-loll at'll paint thi parlour." – I know an odd-job man who will paint your lounge."
loin. lane.
"Leeds Loiners (nickname); dahn yar (down your) loin."
loise. lose.
"I'd rayther loise 'awf nor aw." – I'd rather lose half than all.
lollicker + tung. tongue.
"Shove oot thi lollicker." – Put out your tongue.
long-dog. greyhound.
"E runs as wick (quickly) as a longdog."
looadner. loader.
"Ah's allus t'looadner." – I'm always the loader.
loom-gate. space between two looms.
"Sweep up t'loom-gate."
lop (from Swedish loppa). flea.
"Peert as a lop." – Nimble as a flea.
lopper. cover.
"Thoo's loppert wi'muck." – You're covered with dirt.
louse-comm. small comb for removing head-lice.
"Try this 'ere (this) louse-comm."
love-feeast. prayer-meeting.
"Yon Prims (those Primitive Methodists) are at their love-feeast."
lowk. weed.
"Lowkin' t'wheeat." – Weeding the wheat.
lowp. leap.
"A sheep lowped ower t'waw." – A sheep jumped over the wall.

lowsin'-shower. Shower stopping work for the day.
"Gaa yam (go home): it's a lowsin'-shower."

lowsin'-time. finishing-time.
"It's nigh on (almost) lowsin'-time."

lug. pull.
"It's ower big ti lug." – It's too big to pull.

lug-'oil. ear-hole.
"I'll pelt thi lug-'oil (strike your ear-hole)."

lug-puddin'. troublesome suckling child.
"Thou's a gret (you're a great) lug-puddin'."

lumber. rubbish; trouble.
"E awlus falls i' some mak o' lumber (into some kind of trouble)."

M

mafted. stifled.
"Oppen t'winder – Ah's ommast mafted." – Open the window – I'm almost stifled.

maggie. magpie.
"Maggies is on t'flay-crow (scare-crow)."

maltworm. tippler.
"Yon maltworm's i't'pub." – That tip-pler's in the pub.

mangle. wringer.
"Ton t'mangle." – Turn the wringer.

mardy. spoil child.
"Ya gert soft mardy!" – You great soft spoilt child!

marlock. play mischievously.
"We began marlockin' amung t'desks (among the desks)."

mash. brew.
"Is t'teea mashed yet?" – Is the tea brewed yet?

matter. pus.
"Bust (burst) thi boil an' get t'matter aht."

maungy. peevish, spoilt.
"A gert maungy babby." – A great spoilt baby.

mawk. maggot.
"As far as a mawk."

mawl. handle roughly.
"Dooan't mawl yon fruit."

mawn't. mustn't.
"Ah mawn't grummle." – I mustn't grumble.

mazy. dizzy.
"Them whirligigs (those round-abouts) meks me mazy."

mazzles. measles.
"Oor babby's catched t'mazzles." – Our baby's caught the measles.

meean. mean.
"Ow's ta meean?" – How do you mean?

meeast + mooast. most.
"Meeast o' ya's gannin'." – Most of you are going.

mell. large mallet.
"Clobber t'steean wi' thi mell." – Strike the stone with your mallet

melsh. mild (of weather).
"A melsh neet." – A mild night.

mense. neat.
"She tons (turns) 'er family out mense."

mester. Mr.; master; my husband.
"Mester (Mr.) Smith; lahtle mesters (little masters – in the Sheffield cut-lery trade); I'll call t'mester (my husband)."

meyt. food.
"E gets meyt at's dowther's." – He gets food at his daughter's.

mich. much.
"Women wi' nowt mich on." – Almost naked women.

midden. manure heap.
As meean (mean) as midden-muck."

middlin'. moderate.
"'Ow's trade?" "Nobbut (only) mid-dlin'."

mig. mess, panic.

"Accidents gets me in a reyt (real) mig."

missus. wife.
"Ah'll etta ax t'missus." – I'll have to ask my wife.

mistle. old-fashioned cow-house. See also byre, shippon.
"Try laitin' (seeking) 'im i' t'mistle."

mizzle. drizzle.
"It's just mizzlin' a larl (little) bit."

moggy. cat.
"Why, it's ahr (our) moggy!"

moil. turmoil.
"Tha's gitten in a proper (you have got into a real) moil."

moither. harrass.
"Moithered wi' aw them bairns (by all those children)."

moke. donkey.
"Mokes is on t'sands at Brid." – Donkeys are on Bridlington sands.

monk. a scowl.
"Teycher's getten a monk on." – Teacher is scowling.

monkey. mortgage.
"There's a monkey on ahr 'ahs (our house)."

mooinleet flit. removal at night to avoid the bum-bailey (sheriff's officer).
"They're doin' a mooinleet flit."

mooit. grumble.
"Allus mooitin' abaht summat." – Always grumbling about something.

mowdywarp mole.
"Mowdywarps burrers in t'grund." – Moles burrow into the ground.

muck. dirt (probably from Old Norse myki).
"That's reyt clarted wi' muck." – You're quite daubed with dirt.

muck bods. curlews (e.g. in Holderness).
"We 'eeard (heard) t'muck-bods."

muck-lather. great perspiration.
"'E were all of a muck lather (sweating profusely)."

muckle + mickle. much.
"It's ower muckle." – It's too much.

muck-mense. despoiler.
"Thou ugly muck-mense!" (e.g. to a dog which has fouled a clean room).

muckment. unsuitable literature or talk.
"Give o'er! (Stop it!). It's nowt but muckment."

muck-midden. manure heap.
"Dooan't mak thi belly (don't make your stomach) into a muck-midden."

muckworm. sordid greedy person.
"E's a reyt (real) muckworm, rummagin' in aw that kelter (rubbish)."

mucky. dirty.
"Mucky Willy's (name of a Bradford pub); 'e's muckied 'is ticket (spoilt his chance)."

mud. might.
"It mud a bin wahr." – It might have been worse.

mullock. mess.
"Med a mullock on it." – Made a mess of it.

mun. must.
"Them as corn't wark, mun plan." – Those who can't work, must plan.

N

naff. nave.
"T'wheel's up to t'naff i'sludge."

nark. annoy.
"Shape thissen (i.e. improve your work) or tha'll nark 'im."

neb. bird's beak.
"T'craa (the crow) sharpened 'is neb."

neck-oil. beer.
"Suppin' (drinking) 'is neck-oil."

neea + nooa. no.
"She'll tak neea 'arm." – She'll take no harm.

neeave + neive. fist.
"'E up wi' 'is neeave (raised his fist) an' knocked 'im ovver."

neet. evening; night.
"Midneet (midnight); ah'll sithee (see you) i' t'pub toneet (this evening)."
nesh. delicate, cold.
"Ah feels reyt nesh." – I feel quite cold.
nessy (short for necessary). earth-closed. See also petty, privy.
"It's ahr ton to cleyn t'nessy." – It's our turn to clean the earth-closet.
nevvy. nephew.
"Is nevvy warks i' Bratford." – His nephew works in Bradford.
niggly. miserly.
"T'landlooard seems reyt (quite) niggly."
nip-fig + nip-currant, nip-screw. miser.
"Sam's a reglar nip-fig." – Sam's a real miser.
nivver. nevver.
"Thoo's a nivver-sweeat." – You're a never-sweat (i.e. an idler).
nobbut. only.
"Ah've nobbut yan." – I've only one.
nobdy + neeabody. nobody.
"Nobdy thinks Ah ail owt." – Nobody thinks I'm at all ill.
nog. work doggedly and reliably.
"Ah just keeps noggin' on."
nooaze-'oils. nostrils.
"Mi nooaze-'oils is blocked wi' cowd (cold)."
nor. than.
"Livin's better nor deein." – Living's better than dying.
nous. sense.
"E'll nut (not) do: 'e's got nooa (no) nous."
nowt. nothing.
"Tak (take) nowt an' gie (give) nowt."
numb-yed. fool.
"This joiner's a numb-yed."
nut. not.
"Nut sin Kersmas." – Not since Christmas.

O

ocker. hesitate.
"Shoo (she) ockered an'stammered."
'od. hold.
"Od on a bit!" – Wait a moment.
odd-lads. order of the Odd Fellows.
"Ah were in t'Odd Lads."
'og. potato-clamp.
"We'll mak (make) a 'og i' t'cloise (in the field)."
'oil. Also 'ooal, hole. See bobby-'oil, chip-oil, coil-'oil, saur-'oil.
'olm. low-lying land near a river. Compare 'ing.
Holmfirth and Holme in the West Riding.
'ollin. holly.
"Pricked bi a 'ollin-busk." – Pricked by a holly-bush.
ommast. almost.
"Ah's ommast done for." – I'm almost exhausted.
ony. any.
"Onywheer (anywhere); ony rooad (at any rate); it didn't rain ony (at all)."
'ooam. home. Also 'eeam, yam.
"Bide thissell (stay) at 'ooam."

'oofs. callosities on hands. Compare segs.
"Looka these 'ere 'oofs Ah've get-ten." – Look at these callosities I've got.
'ooin. overwork, harass.
"Fair 'ooined wi' t'job." – Quite over-worked with the task.
oon. oven.
"Shove t'cake i't'oon (into the oven)."
'op-flag. hop-scotch.
"Shoo'll nut lake at 'op-flag." – She'll not play at hop-scotch.
orts. fragments.
"Nowt (nothing) but orts left."

'oss. horse.
"Ploo 'osses is deein' oot." – Plough horses are dying out.

oss. try.
"E nivver osses to do owt." – He never tries to do anything.

outby. towards the mine-shaft bottom.
"T'shift's up (finished): they're gannin' (going) outby."

ower-kessen. overcast.
"T'sky's leeakin' gay ower-kessen." – The sky's looking very overcast.

'owsumivver. however.
"Owsumivver, Ah manished." – However, I managed.

owt. anything.
"Ah've nivver seen owt (never seen anything) like it."

oxter. armpit.
"wi' a fooitball (with a football) tucked under 'is oxter."

P

pace-egg. Easter-egg (connected with paschal).
"Rollin' pace-eggs dahn-'ill (downhill) on Eeaster Sunda (Easter Sunday)."

pap. teat; mother's milk.
"Gie t'bairn some pap." – Give the child some mother's milk.

parkin. cake made of oatmeal and treacle.
"Ah's lookin' forrard to eytin' (eating) some parkin."

parky. chilly.
"Lap thissen up (wrap up); it feels reyt (quite) parky."

parlour. sitting-room.
"Come into t'parlour an' mek thissen at 'ooam (make yourself at home)."

paws. hands.
"Wesh thi mucky paws." – Wash your dirty hands.

pawse. kick.

"E pawsed mi shin."

pay. hit.
"Wheea's bin payin' oor lass?" – Who's been hitting our daughter?

peff. cough gently.
"Peffin' an coughin' aw neet lang (all night long)."

peggy-tub. wash tub.
"Bendin' their back (backs) ovver a peggy-tub."

pent. hard-pressed.
"Ah'm pent for time."

perished. very cold.
"Mi feet's perished." – My feet are freezing.

pesky. annoying.
"A pesky lot o'rubbish."

petty. earth-closet. See also nessy, privy.
"Shoo's on t'petty." – She's on the earth-closet.

peyl. damage.
"Yon fridge is fair peyled abaht (badly damaged)."

pig-'ull. Sty.
"Crooidled (curled) up i' t'pig-'ull."

piggin. lading can.
"Prentices ate their podish (Apprentices ate their porridge) out o' piggins."

pike. to spy.
"Gie ower pikin' at 'er next dooar." – Stop spying on the lady next door to you.

pikel. hay-fork.
"Lift thi pikel 'eigher up." – Lift your hay-fork higher.

pikelet. crumpet.
"a basketful o' muffins an' pikelets.

pincer-tooad. pigeon-toed. Also twilly-tooad.
"Them shoon is ower tight (those shoes are too tight): tha's walkin' pincer-tooad."

pinchers. pincers.
"Wheer's mi pinchers?" – Where are my pincers?

pine. go hungry.
"We mun pine, beg or steyl." – We must go hungry, beg or steal.
pissibed. dandelion.
"Rive aht them pissibeds." – Pull out those dandelions.
pissimer. ant.
"A pissimer's stinged (stung) mi lip."
piss-pot. chamber-pot.
"Teem aht t'piss-pot." – Empty the chamber-pot.
pittle. urinate.
"E's pittled 'is britches." – He's urinated into his trousers.
plodge. paddle.
"Plodgin i' t'beck." – Paddling in the stream.
Plot-neet. Bonfire Neet. See also Bunfire Neet.
"Ah'm feared whenivver (afraid whenever) Plot Neet comes round.
ploo. plough.
"Od t'ploo varra steady." – Hold the plough very steady.
pluck. entrails.
Dusta want mooar pluck?" – do you want some more entrails?
plum. quite.
"Plum wrang (quite wrong); plum noth (due north)."
poddish. porridge.
"Eyt aw thi poddish." – Eat all your porridge.
poggy. swampy, muddy.
"This loin's rayther poggy." – This lane's rather muddy.
poison. poisonous.
"Tooadstools is reyt poison." – Toadstools are very poisonous.
poke. bag.
"Tha's bust t'flour poke." – You've burst the flour bag.
polly. hornless cow.
"Freetened bi a blartin' polly." – Frightened by a bellowing hornless cow.
posser + peggy stick. wooden implement for stirring clothes in wash-tub.
"Use this 'ere posser."
posset. vomit.
"Yon babby's possetin' ageean" – That baby's vomiting again.
posset. warm drink including milk and bread.
"Traycle posset." – Treacle posset.
possnit. saucepan. Compare skillet
"Sup aht a' this owd possnet." – Drink out of this old saucepan.
pouk. stye.
"Bits o' pouks on is een." – Little styes on his eyes.
pow. poll.
"Ev a ow (have a haircut); a carroty pow (head of red hair)."
pow-cat. polecat.
"This shop stinks like a pow-cat." – This place stinks like a polecat.
privy. earth-closet. See also nessy, petty.
"Tha's left t'cannle i' t'privy." – You've left the candle in the earth-closet.
proggle. prod.
"Progglin' abaht i' t'mud." – Prodding into the mud.
puddins. intestines of slaughtered animal.
"Slit oppen (open) t'belly an' leet aht (let out) t'puddins.
pund. pound.
"'E's nowt-a-pound." – He's nothing-a-pound., i.e. worthless.
puther. perspiration.
"All of a puther."
pynot. magpie.
Also nickname for all dwellers in Holme.

R

rammel. rubbish.
"A looad of owd rammel." – A load of

old rubbish.

Ranter + Prim. Primitive Methodist.
"Ah 'ates (I hate) them Ranters."

ranty (-pole). see-saw. See also sway-pole.
"Bairns sat on a ranty." – Children sitting on a see-saw.

ratch. retch.
"'E seemed fair (likely) to ratch 'is inside out."

rattan. rat.
"Thoosans o' rattans." – Thousands of rats.

rawky. raw and misty.
"It's rawky this mooarnin (morning)."

recklin. smallest and weakest of a litter.
"What a poor recklin it is!"

reeak. smoke.
"T' chimneyd reeaks." – The chimney is smoking.

reeasty. rancid.
"Theeas taties is reeasty." – These potatoes are rancid.

renny + rennard. fox.
"They nivver fun t'renny." – They never found the fox.

reyk. reach.
"Reyk me yon fiddle." – Reach me that violin.

reyt + reet. right; very.
"Ton reyt (turn right); it's nut reet (not right); a reet (very) bad warp."

ride-the-mooin. wild dissipated fellow.
"Esta met yon (have you met that) ride-the-mooin?"

rift. belch.
"Parsnips awlus meks me rift." – Parsnips always make me belch.

riggin. ridge of roof.
"Ah'll climm onto t'ahs-riggin." – I'll climb on to the house-ridge.

riggot + riggel. castrated horse.
"This 'ere's (this is) a riggot."

rig-welted. on its back and unable

to rise (of a sheep).
"Yan o t'gimmers is rig-welted." – One of the gimmers is stuck on its back.

rime. hoar-frost.
"We can't mow t'lawn wi' this 'ere (this) rime."

rioobub. rhubarb.
"Ast seed (have you seen) mi fine rioobub?"

rive. pull.
"Rivin' yan anudder's 'air." – pulling one another's hair.

roak. thick mist.
"Lost on t'moor wi' a roak (because of a thick mist)."

roister. lively child.
"Yon babby's a roister." – That baby's lively.

ronce. scramble and climb.
"Thi clooas is tore (your clothes are torn): tha's bin roncin'."

rooad. way.
"Ger aht o' t'rooad (get out of the way); they dooan't boil eggs that rooad."

roopy. hoarse.
"T'babby's getten a roopy cough." – The baby has got a hoarse cough.

rudstake. stake for fastening a cow in the cow-shed.
"Tie yon 'eifer to t'rudstake."

runneers. gym-shoes.
"Doff thi runners." – Take off your gym shoes.

S

sackless. senseless.
"A poor sackless feeal." – A poor senseless fool.

sad. heavy.
"As sad as a dumplin'."

saim. lard.
"Ah'd nowt (I'd nothing) but a bit o' saim to mi breead (bread)."

sam. gather.

"Git them tooils (get those tools) sammed up."

sazur-'oil + suff-'oil. drainage-put in field.

"Teem (pour) t'sludge down t'saur-'oil."

scale. rake.

"Ah've scaled t'fire out." – I've raked out the fire.

scallions. spring onions.

"A big bunch o' scallions."

schooil. school.

"Schooil's loised." – School's finished.

scopperil. naughty child.

"Thoo lahtle (you little) scopperil!"

scrab. steal.

"They scrabbed mi taws." – They stole my marbles.

scraffle. scramble.

"T'ens (the hens) scraffled oot o' t'way o't'cart-wheels."

scrat. scratch.

"Ens'll scrat up owt." – Hens will scratch up anything.

scrooil. crease, crumple.

"Ah've sat on t'nooospapper (newspaper) an' scrooiled it."

scruffle. hoe.

"Git them tonnups scruffled." – Get those turnips hoed.

scud + wheel. halo.

"There's a scud rahnd t'mooin." – There's a halo round the moon.

scuff. scruff.

"E collared me bi t'scuff o' t'neck."

scurf. dandruff.

"Comm oot yon scurf." – Comb out that dandruff.

seemin'- glass + lookin'-glass. mirror.

"Shoo brak t'seemin'-glass." – She broke the mirror.

seet. sight; great deal.

"Eeseet (eyesight); a seet (great deal) o' good luck."

segs. callosities on hands.

"Yon spead's gin me segs." – That spade's given me callosities.

-sen. (South Yorks.) + sell (North Yorks.) self.

"Ah'll drive missen (myself); 'E killed 'issen (himself); They do it all thersens (themselves); Ah'll wesh misell (wash myself)."

set-pot. copper for boiling clothes; container for making stew.

"Clooas weshin i' t'set-pot (clothes being washed in the copper); chuck them cabbish leeaves in (throw those cabbage leaves into) t'set-pot."

shackle. wrist.

"Ah've spreeaned mi shackle." – I've sprained my wrist.

shake-rag. tramp.

"We met a shake-rag on t'rooad (on the road)."

sharn. manure.

"A dose o' thick cow-sharn."

sharra. char-a-bane.

"We went from Cas (Castleford) to Fila (Filey) in a larl (little) sharra."

sheeaf + shaf. sheaf.

"Tee up them sheeaves." – Tie up those sheaves.

shepster. starling. Compare gippy.

"Earken that theer shepster." – Listen to that starling.

shift + shimmy. chemise.

"Shoo warked (she worked) in 'er shift sleeves."

shippon. old-fashioned ow-house. Compare byre, mistle.

"Milkin' t'coos i' t'shippon." – Milking the cows in the cowhouse.

ship's 'usband. man employed by shipowners to supply trawlers.

"Theer t'ship's 'usband stood (standing) on t'quay."

shive. slice.

"A shive o'breead." – A slice of bread.

sholl. slide. Compare slur.

"Is pants sholled roond 'is knees." –

His pants slid round his knees.
shollock. dodge something unpleasant.
"Dooan't shollock it." – Don't dodge it.
shoo. she.
"Shoo's my lass." – She's my girl.
shoo(i)n. shoes.
"Sich 'oils i' mi shooin." – Such holes in my shoes.
shooit. shoot.
"If t'missus natters (if your wife keeps arguing), shooit 'er."
shool. shovel.
"Wheer's mi shool?" – Where's my shovel?
shoop. wild rose-hip.
"Pickin' shoops an' bummelkites." – Picking rose-hips and blackberries.
shutten. shut.
"Neeabody's shutten t'yat." – Nobody has shut the gate.
side. clear.
"Tha mun side t'table." – You must clear the table.
sike + sich. such.
"Sike dree jobs as this." – Such tedious jobs as this.
sile. rain hard.
"It thunnered (thundered) an' then siled down."
sime. straw rope.
"Twist the sime real 'ard."
sin. since, ago.
"Oo lang sin?" – How long since?
sind. rinse.
"Sind me that beeasin oot." – Rinse that basin for me.
singlet. vest.
"Mi 'eart's thumpin agin (against) mi singlet."
sitfast. core of boil. Compare gawk.
"Didta squeeze out t'sitfast?" – Did you squeeze out the core?
skeets (at Filey) + feetle-trees Bridlington. skids for launching

boat.
"Push t'skeets under t'coble."
skell-boose. partition between cow-stalls. See also boskin.
skellered. warped.
Yon dooar's skellered." – That door's warped.
skelp. beat.
"Whisht or Ah'll skelp tha!" – Silence or I'll beat you.
sken. squint.
"Skennin' blin' drunk." – Utterly drunk.
skep. coal-bucket.
"We've neea coils i' t'skep." – We've no coal in the bucket.
skerrick. fragment.
"Not a skerrick left i't'cupboard."
skillet. saucepan. Compare poss-nit.
"Wesh aht this greeasy skillet." – Wash out this greasy saucepan.
skilly. thin gruel.
Summat better nor skilly." – Something better than thin gruel.
skitters. diarrhoea.
"Tha seems t'ev t'skitters." – You seem to have diarrhoea.
skrike. shriek.
"Gie 'im summat to skrike for." – Give him something to shriek about.
skun. bankrupt.
"Ah'm reyt skun." – I'm quite bankrupt.
slang-bang. tangle of fishing lines.
"By! (By God!) What a slang-bang!"
slap out. stick out.
"Stop slappin' out thi tung (tongue) at ivverybody (everybody)."
slape. slippery.
"T'rooads is fearful slape." – The roads are dreadfully slippery.
slape-scope. work-dodger.
"Ah knaws thi (I know you), slape-scope!"
slape-tongued. smooth-talking,

hypocritical.

"Dooan't trust 'er: shoo (she's) slape-tongued."

slart. splash.

"Rain's slartin on t'winders." – Rain is splashing onto the windows.

sleck + smudge. coal-dust.

Dooan't put sooa mich sleck on." – Don't put on so much coal-dust.

sleck. slake.

"Mooar yal! Ah's nut 'awf slecked yit." – More ale! I'm not half slaked yet.

sley. that part of the loom which draws the thread.

"Summat's wrang wi' t'sley." – Something's wrong with the sley.

slinkman. knacker.

"That coo'll etta gan (cow willl have to go) to t'slinkman."

Slodder. Splash.

"Deean't slodder thi poddish" – Don't splash your porridge.

slotchin'-oil. place allowing heavy drinking.

"Yon club's a reyt (real) slotchin'- oil."

sluff. top and tail.

"sluffin' gooisegogs." – Topping and tailing gooseberries.

slur. slide. Compare sholl.

"Slurrin' on t'frozzen pond." – Sliding on the frozen pond.

slutch. mud.

"Yon trod (that path)'ll leead thi sooa deep into t'slutch."

sluther. slip, slide.

"E sluthered off t'roof into a tub o' swill."

sluther-guts. excessive drinker.

"Yon sluther-guts is still i' t'snug." – That excessive drinker is still in the pub parlour.

sluthery. slimy.

"Sluthery rooads." – Slimy roads.

slutter-puddin'. sloven.

"Stir thissen, tha slutter-puddin'!" – Wake up, sloven!

smit. mark sheep.

"T'lambs is aw smitted." – The lambs are all marked.

smithereens. fragments.

"It's brokken to smithereens." – It's broken into fragments.

smittle. infect.

"Dooan't lake wi' 'im (don't play with him): 'e'll smittle thi."

smoot-'ooal. hole in the hedge, etc., to let sheep through.

"T'owd tup (the old ram)'s been through this smoot-'ooal."

snagger. hedging-bill.

"Fotch mi snagger." – Fetch my hedging-bill.

snap. light meal.

"Tha's etten aw mi snap." – You've eaten all my lunch.

snavvled. blocked.

"Mi nooas-'oils is aw snavvled up." – My nostrils are quite blocked.

sneck. latch.

"Lift t'dooar-sneck." – Lift the door-latch.

sneck-lifter. price of a drink. i.e. admission to a pub.

"Canta gimmi (can you give me) a sneck-lifter?"

sneead. snood.

"Fix t'sneeads to t'fishin'-line."

snicket. alleyway. Compare gin-nel.

"Aht o'seet dahn t'snicket." – Out of sight down the alleyway.

snickle. rabbit-snare.

"Copped in a snickle." – Caught in a rabbit-snare.

snipe. chide.

"Ah'ed to snipe 'er." – I had to chide her.

snob. shoemaker.

"Tak thi beeats to t'snob." – Take your boots to the shoemaker.

snod. smooth.

"Shive 'im cloise an' snod." – Cut his hair close and smooth.

snot. nasal mucus.
"Ah's (I am) full o'snot wi' this cowd (cold)."

snot-rag. pocket-handkerchief.
"Dooan't sniff – use thi snot-rag." – Don't sniff: use your handkerchief.

snowen. snowed.
"It's snowen aw t'rooad 'ere." – It has snowed all the way here.

snuff. top and tail gooseberries.
"Ere, Alice, 'elp thi mum wi' this snuf-fin'."

snug. small private room in an inn.
"Ah awlus teks mi mates into t'snug." – I always take my companions into the snug.

sog. work hard.
"Soggin' away wi' a file." – Toiling with a file.

sooin. soon.
"They left ower sooin." – They left too soon.

soss. lap.
"Kittlin's sossin' at their milk." – Kittens lapping their milk.

spane. wean.
"Ah spaned ahr babby this wek." – I weaned our baby this week.

sparrer-farts. freckles. Compare fern-tickles.
"Why, they're nobbut sparrer-farts!" – Why, they're only freckles!

speead. spade.
"Wheer's mi speead?" – Where's my spade?

spell. splinter; rung of ladder.
"Ah've getten a spell (got a splinter) i' mi 'and; watch that brokken spell (broken rung)."

spetch. repair.
"Canta spetch a chap's britches' seeat?" – Can you repair the seat of a man's trousers?

spew-faced. white-faced.
"What's flayed yon spew-faced lass?" – What has frightened that white-faced girl?

speyk. speak.
"Speyk up, Ah corn't ear thi." – Speak up, I can't hear you.

spice. sweets. Compare goodies.
"Gawpin' in aw t'spice-shops." – Staring into all the sweetshops.

spinnerdick. spinning top.
"Ast sin mi spinnerdick?" – Have you seen my spinning top?

spittal. shuttlecock.
"We've lost us spittal." – We've lost our shuttlecock.

splawder-legged. astride. Also straddle/striddle-legged, striddlin'.
"Stannin' splawder-legged at t'dooar to keep me aht."

spooin. spoon.
"A larl tayspooin." – A little teaspoon.

spretch. crack (of eggs hatching).
"They're spretchin' nice." – They're cracking nicely.

sprottle-footed. splay-footed.
"Dooan't laugh cos shoo's sprottle-footed." – Don't laugh because she's splay-footed.

spuggy. sparrow.
"A chirrupy lahl spuggy." – A chirruply little sparrow.

spunk. strength, courage. Compare bant.
"Spunk (courage) enough to speyk aht (speak out)."

squab. old-fashioned sofa.
"Lay thi doon on t'squab." – Lie down on the sofa.

staggarth. stackyard.
"A staggarth full o'cooarn." – A stackyard full of corn.

stang + beeam. beam.
"Propped up bi yak stangs." – Propped up by oak beams.

starve-naked. stark-naked.
"Don summat: tha's starve-naked." – Put something on: you're stark-naked.

staupins. hoof-marks.

"See them staupins?" – Do you see those hoof-marks?

stee. ladder.
"Climm this stee." – Climb this ladder.

steg. gander.
"As teeaf as an aad steg." – As tough as an old gander.

steggle. stagger.
"A young stegglin' foil." – A young staggering foal.

stem. leazve unmilked.
"Stemmin' a coo's wicked." – Leaving a cow unmilked is wicked.

stepmother. loose piece of skin near fingernail. Compare idleback.
"Stop bitin thi stepmother." – Stop biting your loose skin.

steven. order.
"That coit's stevened." – That coat is ordered.

steyl. long-handle.
"Besom steyl." – Besom handle.

stiddy. anvil.
"Of it on this 'ere stiddy." – Hold it on this anvil.

stilt. handle of plough.
"Atween a pair o' ploo-stilts." – Between a pair of plough handles.

stirk. smalll bullock.
"Fratchin' ower t'price of a stirk." Arguing over the price of a small bullock.

stobber. rug-needle.
"Ah've fun mi stobber." – I've found my needle.

stoop. gate-post.
"Restin' on a stoop i' t'loin (in the lane)."

stot. bull.
"A stot gat out o' t'yat." – A bull got out of the gate.

stowed. full.
"Eytin' Yorkshire pud while thoo's stowed." – Eating Yorkshire pudding until you are full.

stower. stake.

"Poo up a stower." – Pull up a stake.

strang. strong.
"Ah feels gay strang." – I feel very strong.

streea. straw.
"Ony aad streea'll deea." – Any old straw will do.

strickle. whetstone.
"Mowers mun tek a strickle." – Mowers must take a whetstone.

suck. ploughshare.
"This ploo needs a noo suck." – This plough needs a new share.

summat. something.
"Summat's up." – Something is the matter.

sup. drink.
"Suppin' us teea." – Drinking our tea.

swad. pod. Compare cod.
"Like peys i' wun swad." – Like peas in one pod.

swammed. swam.
"T'milk swammed under t'armcheer." – The milk ran under the armchair.

swath. bacon-ring.
"Yo (you)'d better cut t'swath off, it's ower (too) tough."

sway-pole. see-saw. Compare ranty (-pole).
"Dooan't let thi toddler run under t'sway-pole."

sweal. burn fiercely.
"Moor fires swealin wi' t'wind." – Moor fires burning fiercely with the wind.

sweear. swear.
"Sitha, dooan't sweear." – Look, don't swear.

swelt. overcome with heat.
"It's aneeaf ti swelt onybody." – It's enough to stifle anybody.

swite. whittle.
"Dooan't swite yon pencil to bits." – Don't whittle that pencil to bits.

swop-shop. second-hand shop.
"Ah selled it to a swop-shop." – I sold it to a second-hand shop.

sword. bacon-rind.
"Cut t'sword off t'beeacon." – Cut the rind off the bacon.

T

tally. together.
"Yon's 'is tally-woman (his mistress); they're livin' tally (together but unmarried)."

tank. cow's urine in cow-house drain.
"Tank smells middlin' bad." – Cow's uring smells fairly bad.

t**art.** girl.
"A fine tart." – A good-looking girl (not necessarily immoral).

taw. marble.
"Lakin' at taws i' t'gutter." – Playing at marbles in the gutter.

teea. tea.
"Sup this 'ere teea." – Drink this tea.

ted. spread.
"Teddin' noo-mown 'ay." – Spreading new-mown hay.

teem. pour.
"T'rain teemed down; teem out." – I'm dry (thirsty)."

tell-tale-tit. tale-bearer.
"You telled on me, tell-tale-tit!" – You told of me, tell-tale!

that. so.
"We could 'ave etten (eaten) a dog, we was that 'ungry."

that. indeed.
"Ah is, that." – I am indeed.

thee. you.
"E thees yer." – He calls you 'thee'.

them. those.
"Them lads (those boys); them's them (those are they)."

thible. porridge-stick.
"Stir t'podish wi' this thible." – Stir the porridge with this stick.

thimmle. thimble.
"Wheer's yon thimmle o' thine?" – Where's that thimble of yours?

thin. cold (of weather).
"It's reyt thin toneet." – It's very cold tonight.

think on. remember.
"E can nivver think on." – He can never remember.

thoil. endure, stand.
"Ah corn't thoil red 'air." – I can't stand red hair.

thoo, thou, tha. you.
"Ow's thoo gettin' on lad?" – How are you getting on, boy?

thrang. busy.
"Booath on us is desperate thrang." – We are both very busy.

threead-bobbin. cottom-reel.
"Giz anudder threead-bobbin." – Give me another cotton-reel.

threeap. argue.
"E'll threeap black's white." – He'll argue that black is white.

throit. throat.
"Nobdy'll ax if yo've a throit." – Nobody will ask whether you are thirsty.

throstle. thrush.
"Earken yon (listen to that) lovely throstle singin'."

throttle. throat. Compare throit.
"Teem it down thy throttle." – Pour it down your throat.

thrum. waste threads.
"Mind ivvery (beware every) knot an' thrum."

thrummer. threepenny-bit
"Ah've fun a thrummer." – I've found a threepenny-bit.

thrush-lice. wood-lice.
"That baulk's full o' thrush-lice." – That beam's full of wood-lice.

thrutch. thrust, squeeze.
"We thrutched into t'pub." – We squeezed into the pub.

Thump. local holiday.
"Five year come 'Alifax Thump Sunda." – Five years next Halifax Thump Sunday.

thunner. thunder.
"Thunner an' leetnin'." – Thunder and lightning.

tiddlers. minnows.
"Catchin' tiddlers i' jam-jars." – Catching minnows in jam-jars.

tift. pant.
"She's badly, she's nivver done tiftin'." – She's ill, she never stops panting.

tig. children's game of touch.
"Ah catched 'em aw at tig." – I caught them all at tig.

till. to. Compare tiv.
"Thi breakfast's ready: come till it." – Your breakfast's ready: come to it.

tippletailin. somersaulting.
"Ah went tippletailin' ovver." – I went head-over-heels.

titivate. make oneself pretty.
"Shoo's titivatin' ersen up." – She's making herself pretty.

tit(ty). nipple, breast.
"Let t'babby snoozle to its titty." – Let the baby snuggle to its nipple.

tiv. to. Compare till.
"Gan up tiv 'im an ax." – Go up to him and ask.

tivvy. dance about.
"T'lasses is awlus tivvying aboot." – The girls are always dancing about.

toft. rowing-boat seat.
"Sit thi doon i' t'toft." – Sit in the seat.

toit. busy.
"Keep 'im i'toit." – Keep him busy.

tomorn. tomorrow.
"Get it deean bi tomorn." – Get it done by tomorrow.

tommy-owt. odd-job man. Compare daytalman, knockaboot.
"Tommy-owts is (are) good 'elp at 'arvest."

tommy-squealer. the swift.
"We seed (saw) a tommy-squealer."

tom-tellalegs + tommy-spinner. daddy-longlegs, crane-fly.
"There's a tom-tellalegs on t'winder."

– There's a daddy-longlegs on the window.

ton. turn.
"Ah tonned t'parlour oot." – I cleaned out the parlour.

tonnap. turnip.
"tonnap-bashin." – Pulling turnips.

tooith (S.W. Yorks.) + teeath (North. Yorks.). tooth.
"Asta getten tooithwark (have you got toothache)?; this teeath'll etta come oot (this tooth will have to come out)."

toot. (Anglo-Saxon totian "espy"). pry into things.
"Shoo's awlus tootin'." – She's always prying.

top-coit. overcoat.
"Cowd enough for a top-coit." – Cold enough for an overcoat.

toppin'. forelock (of a person or horse).
"Yon daft barber's cut mi toppin'." – That silly barber's cut my forelock.

traycle. treacle.
"Giz anudder traycle-sop." – Give me another sup of treacle.

trod. footpath.
"Keep on t'reyd trod." – Keep on the right footpath.

trollops. sloven.
"Shoo's a mucky trollops." – She's a dirty sloven.

trones. weighing-scales.
"Bring t'trones an' weigh this 'ere cabbish (this cabbage)."

troughin'. gutter.
"T'troughin's leeakin'." – The gutter's leaking.

trump. break wind.
See also fart, let off.

tun-dish + tunnel. funnel.
"Teem it through a tun-dish." – Pour it through a funnel

tuner. weaving overlooker.
"Billy were a tuner." – Billy was an overlooker.

61

turds. animal droppings.
"Sam yon 'oss-turds up." – Gather that horse-manure.

twang-tooad + twiddy/twilly-toed. pigeon-toed.
"Sithee, 'e's twang-tooad." – Look, he's pigeon toed.

twinter (from 2 + winter). 2-year-old sheep.
"Mooast on 'em's twinters." – Most of them are 2-year-olds.

twitch. couch-grass.
"T'field's a regular twitch-bed." – The field's a real couch-bed.

twitch-bell. earwig. Compare forkin'-robin, jinny-spinner.
"As brahn as a twitch-bell." – As brown as an earwig.

two-double. bowed from age or infirmity.
"E walks two-double." He walks bent.

two-three. few.
"A two-three wik sin." – A few weeks ago.

tyke. general term for a shrewd Yorkshireman.
"An owd Yorkshire tyke." – An old Yorkshire tyke.

U

'uggin-booan. hip-bone.
"Mi'uggin-booan's givin' me gip." – My hip-bone's very painful.

ullert. owl(et). troublesome child.
"Come on, yer lahtle ullert!" – Come on, you little mischief!

'um. low.
"Coos 'ummin i' t'shippon." – Cows lowing in the cowshed.

'ummer. the devil!
"ummer ter (down with) muckin' aht osses (horses) ivvery day!"

up. raise.
"She upped wi' t'claht (raised the dish-cloth) an' swiped 'im across

t'chops (cheeks)."

up-grown. grown-up.
"Mi childer's aw up-grown an' set-tled." – My children are all grown-up and settled.

uppins. shoe-uppers.
"These 'ere uppins is cracked." – These uppers are cracked.

urchin. hedgehog.
"Urchins ligs 'id i' 'winter." – Hedgehogs lie hidden in winter.

us. our.
"Wun of us own." – One of our own.

'utch. snuggle.
"Shoo 'utched cloise to me." – She snuggled close to me.

V

various veins + varry coarse veins. varicose veins.
"Ah suffers real bad from varry coarse veins." – I suffer very badly from varicose veins.

varry + varra. very.
"Varry like kthee." – Very like you.

voider. clothes-basked.
"T'voider's tumbled ovver." – The clothes-basket's tumbled over.

W

waffy + waller, walsh. insipid.
"This soup's ower waffy." – This soup's too insipid.

wag. play truant.
"E's waggin' again."

wake. weak. Also wankly.
"as wake as watter (water)."

wakken. (a)waken.
"Lad, thoo's asleep. Wakken up!" – Boy, you're asleep. Awaken!

wankly. weak. Compare wake.
"Oor legs feel wankly yit." – Out legs still feel weak.

waarda. work-day.

"Shoo's awlus warkin', Sundas an wardas." – She's always working, Sundays and workdays.

wark. ache.
"Creased wi' belly-wark." – Doubled up with stomache-ache.

warse + wahr. worse.
"For better nor warse." – For better or worse.

wath. ford.
"Bairns plodgin' doon i' t'wath." – Children paddling down in the ford.

watter. water.
"T'watter's silin' off t'eeasins." – The water's pouring off the house-eaves.

weean't. won't.
"She weean't scrub t'fleear." – She won't scrub the floor.

weel. well.
"They're varry weel-off." – They're very rich.

weet. wet.
"Sodden wi t'weet." – Soaking wet.

wesh. wash.
"Ah mun wesh t'clooas." – I must wash the clothes.

wether-'og. male sheep before its first shearing.
"Clip (shear) them wether-'ogs."

weyver. weaver.
"Bob's a champion weyver." – Bob's an excellent weaver.

wham. marshy land.
"T' wham's seea mortal sumpy." – The marsh is so very boggy.

whang. boot-lace.
"Mi booit-whang's brokken." – My bootlace is broken.

wheer. where.
"Wheer's mi man?" – Where's my mother?

whemmle. topple.
"T'stack mawn't whemmle ower." – The stack mustn't topple over.

whemmly. wobbly.
"This 'ere bowl is reyt whemmly." – This bowl is very wobbly.

while. until.
"Wait while Ah leets mi pipe." – Wait until I light my pipe.

whinge-fart. constant complainer.
"Stop whingin', yer lahtle whinge-fart." – Stop whining, you little complainer (to a child).

wick. alive.
"Fayther's deead but Mother's wick." – Father's dead but Mother's alive.

wick. quick (of the nail).
"It's bitten dahn to t'wick." – It's bitten down to the quick.

winter-'edge. clothes-horse.
"Rahnd t'fire were a winter-'edge." – Round the fire was a clothes-horse.

wishin. cushion.
"Fotch us a wishin." – Fetch me a cushion.

wockery. weak.
"Ah feels rare wockery." – I feel very weak.

wots. oats.
"Osses eyts plenty o' wots." – Horses eat plenty of oats.

wrang. wrong.
"She's t'wrang side oot today." – i.e. She's in a bad mood today.

wun. wound.
"Esta wun up t'case-clock?" – Have you wound the grandfather clock?

wun + yan. one.
"Wun day (one day); yan of oor mates (one of our friends)."

wunce + yance. once.
"Wunce a day; Ah were 'ere (was here) yance."

Y

yak + ooak. oak.
"A yak cubbert." – An oak cupboard.

yal. ale.
"Ah've drunk a quart o' yal." – I've drunk a quart of ale.

yam. home. Also 'eeam, 'ooam.
"E's gan yam." – He's gone home.

yammer. chatter.
*"Bairns is awlus yammerin'." –
Children are always chattering.*
yark. jerk.
*"T'dentist yarked mi tooith aht." –
The dentist jerked out my tooth.*
yat + yet, geeat. gate.
"Oppen t'yat." – Open the gate.
yawrks. knee-straps .
*"Ah mostlins weears yawrks." – I
generally wear knee-straps.*
yeld. arrangement of loops in a
weaving machine.
"Weyvers (weavers) see to t'yeld."
yest. yeast.
*"Three penn'orth o' yest." – Three
penny-worth of yeast.*
yigh. yes (contradictory).
*"Yigh, 'e does. Thoo's wrang." Yes,
he does. You're wrong.*
yocken. to gulp.

*"sitha! 'E's yockenin' it dahn." – Look!
He's gulping it down.*
yon(d). that.
*"E's a sharp 'un, is yond." – He's a
clever one, is that man.*
yonderly. ill (as if about to go to
heaven).
*"Tha's lookin' yonderly." – You look
critically ill.*
yop. farm labourer.
*"E warks as a yop." – He works as a
farm labourer.*
Yorkshire, in go Yorkshire. pay
one's share.
*"They med us go Yorkshire." – They
made us pay our share.*
Yorkshireman. fly drowned in ale.
*"Ere's a Yorkshireman, sitha!" –
Look, here's a drowned fly!*

"There now, isn't that more manly?"